Praise for *Simply Open*

"If we but 'simply open' ourselves, Greg Paul shows us how the whole world is full of God. This is a book that will stay with you for life."

—LEONARD SWEET, BEST-SELLING AUTHOR, PROFESSOR
(DREW UNIVERSITY, GEORGE FOX UNIVERSITY), AND
CHIEF CONTRIBUTOR TO SERMONS.COM

"Greg Paul writes with the language of a poet, the compassion of a pastor and the insight of a philosopher. *Simply Open* will inspire and inform you in new ways that will deepen your spiritual journey and relationship with God."

—MARK SANBORN, BEST-SELLING AUTHOR OF *THE FRED FACTOR* AND *YOU DON'T NEED A TITLE TO BE A LEADER*

"Greg Paul shows God's tender involvement with the gritty realities of life. Greg's hard-won wisdom and biblical and theological insight are expressed through lavish love of language, a telling eye for stories, and lush descriptive passages. This potent combination makes the book a sacrament."

—ARTHUR BOERS, AUTHOR OF *THE WAY IS MADE BY WALKING: A PILGRIMAGE ALONG THE CAMINO DE SANTIAGO*

"*Simply Open* is an inspiring and insightful book. It practically addresses the need followers of Jesus have for contemplation in the midst of busy lives. If each of us were to take some of this to heart, our Christian communities would be more transforming and be healthier places."

—DAVID EDWARDS, BISHOP OF THE
ANGLICAN DIOCESE OF FREDERICTON

SIMPLY
OPEN

SIMPLY OPEN

A GUIDE TO EXPERIENCING
GOD IN THE EVERYDAY

GREG PAUL

NELSON
BOOKS

An Imprint of Thomas Nelson

Published in Nashville, Tennessee, by Nelson Books, an imprint of Thomas Nelson. Nelson Books and Thomas Nelson are registered trademarks of HarperCollins Christian Publishing, Inc.

Published in association with the literary agency of Daniel Literary Group, LLC, Nashville, TN 37215.

Thomas Nelson titles may be purchased in bulk for educational, business, fund-raising, or sales promotional use. For information, please e-mail SpecialMarkets@ThomasNelson.com.

Library of Congress Cataloging-in-Publication Data

Paul, Greg, 1958-
  Simply open : a guide to experiencing God in the everyday / Greg Paul.
    pages cm
  Includes bibliographical references.
  ISBN 978-1-4002-0668-1
  1. Spiritual life--Christianity. I. Title.
  BV4501.3.P38575 2015
  248.4--dc23
                          2014023479

Printed in the United States of America

14 15 16 17 18 RRD 6 5 4 3 2 1

*For all the soul-hungry strivers, the white-knucklers,
the duty-bound, and the driven, who, like me, long
to let go and open wide to a new world of grace*

Contents

I

The Path to Openness

To open is to unveil, to unlock, to unclench, to invite. To create passage, to begin. Openness means generosity and truthfulness and clarity and spaciousness and fearless receptiveness and a willingness to be moved.

An open door invites me to enter, signals my release, tells me I am free to come and go. An open vista lets me see clearly into the distance, and it tantalizes me with possibility. Open water offers a sailor the liberty to choose a course unconstrained by land or shoal, an infinite choice of destination—and the sobering recognition of dependence upon wind, water, and current. A gift, upon being opened, reveals not only the nature of the item previously hidden but also the thoughtfulness of and the blessing conferred by the giver.

An open jar of olives is the beginning of a feast; an open bottle of wine, the start of celebration. The sight, the sound, the smell, the taste, the touch. The opening bars of a song or the opening paragraphs of a book are the commencement of a shared creative journey.

An open face is honest, humble—the expression of a person

secure in oneself and desirous of finding the good in others. An open heart is warm and tender, ready for friendship. An open mind is generous, engaging, respectful of others, eager to grow and learn. Open arms offer welcome and comfort. An open spirit receives and perceives without condemnation.

An open society is one that values transparency over secrets. It chooses the vulnerability of welcoming the stranger over the security of exclusivity. It celebrates the richness of diversity over the comfort of homogeneity. It embraces new or different perspectives rather than defending tired dogmas. It does not rush to judgment.

Openness requires courage. By its nature it diminishes certainty and requires faith; it dismantles the mighty fortresses of ego and privilege, leaving one armed instead with the flimsy weapons of hope and love. Openness takes captive one's own private agenda, binding it to the needs and dreams of others.

The one who is truly open desires to be known, unveiled, right down to every blemish, each unrecognized strength.

The one who is truly open desires also to know, even if the knowing destroys cherished illusions. This is good, but it may also be terrifying.

"It is a fearful thing," said the writer of the letter to the Hebrews, "to fall into the hands of the living God" (10:31 KJV).

Fearful, yes. But where safer? And where in this universe could one find greater excitement, deeper fulfillment, more enduring peace, a richer joy? This is why God seeks to cleave me, pierce me "to the division of soul and of spirit, of joints and of marrow, and discerning the thoughts and intentions of the heart" (Heb. 4:12 ESV). Not to harm, but to heal. To open a path.

God is the Great Openness. Surely Jesus is the evidence of this: the Omnipotent becomes powerless; the Omnipresent binds himself to a point in time, a geographical and cultural place, a specific person within the narrow confines of history; the Omniscient bends every aspect of that infinite genius to the purpose of being known. Every created thing is a revelation, and "no creature is hidden from his sight, but all are naked and exposed to the eyes of him to whom we must give account" (Heb. 4:13 ESV).

If, then, openness is a path inward to the very core of my own being, the path leads also outward from that core to the heart of God.

I want to be free, but not without direction. I want to be humble, but not insecure. I want to be vulnerable *and* fearless. I desire simplicity, but the kind that is profound rather than naïve. I want to *know* God, and myself, and others.

I want to be open. But such openness is not easy.

As much as I might want to, I cannot simply fling some internal door open and be instantly flooded with the insight, humility, serenity, and intimacy with God and others that I crave. Seeking such openness, I find, is more like a battle, one in which I have dug trenches and foxholes, built bunkers and fortresses, to protect myself.

Ironically, the strongholds I have built for protection have proven to be my dungeon.

Openness has many enemies: fear, weariness, insecurity, past traumas and disappointments, pride, selfishness. These and many others are the thick walls behind which we hide, behind which we are trapped. They may manifest themselves in our lives as variously as life-dominating drives to succeed, dependence on drugs or alcohol, arrogance or low self-esteem (or both), habitual self-sabotage, or self-aggrandizement.

Or busyness. We are, all of us, deeply hungry for spiritual life. We long to really work our spiritual muscles and grow strong. But we, too, are overwhelmed by successive waves: financial challenges, work or educational expectations, social imperatives, the never-ending swell of entertainment options, the needs of family and friends.

I'm a husband, father to four, and stepfather to three children; a sadly neglectful son to my very sweet mother; a brother twice over. I am a pastor, fund-raiser, teacher, author, mentor, networker, advocate, and outreach worker. I travel regularly and speak about God and justice. I have played in the same band for almost three decades. I provide some coaching and advice to people across the continent who are nurturing communities similar to Sanctuary. My life is full of people and activities.

Like you, I'm busy. Busy, busy. Look, I'm not bragging—most people I know are just as busy or busier, and they could easily produce lists much like mine.

Of all the enemies that bar the path to becoming increasingly more open, this one—*busyness*—may loom largest. Busyness is highly valued and deeply entrenched in our Western culture, whether it's a fruitful busyness or not. Busyness is the mark of importance: an executive who isn't run off her feet is probably on the way out; professionals and tradespeople of all sorts work long hours and add regular training to upgrade their status; any gathering of religious leaders features the proud comparison of crammed schedules; parents moan about the hectic rounds that must be made to get the kids to school, sports activities, music and dance lessons . . .

Busyness, perhaps more than anything else, affirms our value. It tells us that we're important, needed, or desired. Unchallenged busyness might be slowly strangling our souls.

But busyness for an increasing number of ordinary people isn't all ego-driven. A 2004 study conducted in Toronto, my hometown, revealed that a single parent needed to work *two* full-time minimum-wage jobs—a seventy-two-hour week, not including transportation time—just to reach the poverty line.[1] A great many executives and managers know that unless they routinely labor long past the day's official end, they'll lose their jobs to someone hungrier. The escalating cost of living and the demands of a marketplace whose sole focus is ever-increasing profits constantly require more and more from workers at all levels.

Busyness of this sort isn't going to go away. For many years, I've listened to friends express their frustration at trying to deepen their spiritual lives while keeping up with the demands of work, family, worshipping communities, and other responsibilities. Many people who are successful in their work lives, dedicated worshippers who may be wonderful parents, spouses, and friends, feel like spiritual failures because the majority of their time and creative energy must be submitted to the goals of a corporation or financial institution—goals they feel are essentially meaningless, or worse, with which they feel they are in conflict.

Some are fortunate enough to work in professions that are inherently meaningful and whose value is widely affirmed: health care professionals, teachers, pastors, child and elder care workers, social workers, artists. But even they find the urgency of the demands they face and the fast pace of contemporary life leave little space for spiritual contemplation.

The group with which I have the most natural affinity, because I am one of them, is made up of people who have become activists for justice—gospel justice, which seeks to set people free from spiritual, economic, racial, social, physical, or emotional oppression, in the name of Jesus. My colleagues and I have the great luxury of living each workday in pursuit of spiritual enterprise. We get to read Scripture, pray, even preach or share communion. You would think we'd all be full-blown contemplatives, deeply rooted in lives of intimate prayer and quiet scriptural reflection.

Not so. The rate of burnout in my corner of the vineyard is astonishingly high. Although we may think we're okay because, after all, we're doing God's work—aren't we?—we too often think so right up until something goes drastically wrong. We are so driven by the desperate need of the people among whom we work that it may even seem wrong, somehow, to take time to care for ourselves as well. If it comes down to an hour spent in listening for the voice of God, or that same hour devoted, for instance, to getting a homeless person into housing—especially in the dead of winter—it's usually no contest.

The sheer volume of need overwhelms us. Lives hang in the balance. The more those of us from privileged backgrounds come to love people whose lives have been wrecked from the start, the angrier and more frustrated we are likely to become about the successive waves of injustice that roll over them—waves that we can alter about as successfully as a handful of bodies standing in the surf can divert an ocean's breakers.

Anger is not a good center from which to live a spiritual life. Neither is frustration nor self-condemnation nor soul-numbing weariness. And the demands of even an ordinarily busy life war against our ability to address such wounds, to find a healthy center from which we can live joyful, fruitful lives.

———

These are not new problems. For thousands of years, some spiritual seekers of most faiths have withdrawn from secular life into monasteries, convents, or hermitages, or they have gone on pilgrimages or spirit quests for the purpose of seeking enlightenment, liberation, or a deeper connection with God. Sadhus, ascetic Hindu monks, sometimes spend years wandering homeless and naked, with only a bowl for begging. In most North American First Nations traditions, a spirit quest marks the passage from childhood to adulthood.

Occasionally, the desire for spiritual reality has led seekers to questionable extremes. Saint Simeon Stylites, a Christian monk of the fifth century, is famous for having lived about forty years on a small platform on top of a pillar—as well as torturing himself in a disconcerting number of other ways. Even the people of his time realized his approach might not be entirely sane. Long before he climbed atop the pillar, he had been asked to leave a monastery because of the extremity of his disciplines.[2]

But there is no doubt that true contemplatives have given great gifts to our world. Thomas à Kempis, Julian of Norwich, John of the Cross, Teresa of Ávila, Brother Lawrence, and many others—the fruits of their years of cloistered reflection continue to be precious hundreds of years later. Benedict of Nursia and Ignatius of Loyola developed rules and exercises that still shape communities and individual lives around the world. Their mantle has been worn in our own era by people such as Jean Vanier, Henri Nouwen, Richard Rohr, Kathleen Norris, Thomas Merton, and others.

These are all Catholic followers of Jesus. There's a surprising paucity of contemplatives among Protestants by comparison, and many of those have been profoundly influenced by Catholic writers; but most other spiritual traditions have similar contemplative exemplars.

Most of these great contemplatives, however, have lived lives in which they were able to combine spiritual vocation with "employment." Few of us are able to afford that luxury, if such it can be called, and fewer still have any sense of calling to the rigors and restrictions of a life in orders. Secession from the world is not an option for the vast majority of us. For many, myself included, it would be an abandonment of God's calling on their lives as workers, spouses, parents, and as members of various kinds of community,[3] as that calling is precisely about engagement with the world around us.

How then, when we find ourselves trapped inside the thick walls we have built, can we find a path that allows us to become increasingly open to the voice of God?

Jesus lamented our condition, quoting the words of Isaiah:

> *For this people's heart has become calloused;*
> *they hardly hear with their ears,*
> *and they have closed their eyes.*
> *Otherwise they might see with their eyes,*
> *hear with their ears,*
> *understand with their hearts*
> *and turn, and I would heal them.*

But blessed are your eyes, because they see, and your ears because they hear. (Matt. 13:15–16)

It's encouraging to know that if we turn, God will heal us— open our ears and eyes and hearts. And, as the apostle Paul teaches us, we are not without resource to break out of the fortress-prisons we have constructed around ourselves: "The weapons we fight with are not the weapons of the world. On the contrary, they have divine power to demolish strongholds" (2 Cor. 10:4).

We are not helpless. We can choose to turn, to fight. We can take a new and life-giving path.

I want to offer such a path, a contemplative path toward the simple openness we've been thinking about, based on the intentional exercise of our five senses, our minds, and our hearts. Our senses, minds, and hearts are completely portable, with us all the time. We can't even leave them behind, as I do routinely with my keys and cell phone. The world around us is, well, *around* us—always accessible. Seems like a match made in heaven.

———

If our senses are the means by which our inner selves perceive the realities that surround us, they are also passages through which the Divine may enter our minds and hearts and take up residence. This Visitor, who longs to abide, is unfailingly gracious, and he will not trespass where he is uninvited. The wider we open the doors, the more deeply he abides.

This path is so simple that you can integrate it into the most complex schedule and pick it up again immediately if you forget about it for weeks at a time. It's also flexible enough to use as the basis for times of planned spiritual retreat, should you have that opportunity. However, retreat is a measured withdrawal from the world for a short while; the main intent of this contemplative path is to help us really pay attention to the busy world we must inhabit most of the time, and so experience the presence of the Spirit of God within it.

About the only thing this path requires is a desire to become spiritually open—open to God, to yourself, and to others.

By developing an intentional, increasing awareness of what we are *already registering* through our physical senses, our minds, and our hearts, we will allow God to open us up in four different ways:

Releasing,
Receiving,
Becoming,
Doing.

The first thing that happens when we open up is that we *release* our hold on previous perceptions—judgments, opinions, attitudes. Those perceptions may stay or they may go, but we must relinquish our control of them.

By letting go, we free ourselves to *receive* new perceptions, understanding, wisdom. Sometimes we may receive previously held perceptions again, proving their worth, or we may receive them in a new way—see them from a new angle, or detect a flavor or aroma we hadn't noticed before.

New perceptions, understanding, and wisdom change us. When we are conscious that we have received this new awareness as a gift from God, it opens us up to *become* more truly who and what he has made us to be. Slowly, we "are being transformed into his image with ever-increasing glory, which comes from the Lord, who is the Spirit" (2 Cor. 3:18).

Becoming inevitably bears fruit in *doing*. When we are truly open to being transformed, our motivations change, and we *do*—not out of societal expectation or peer pressure or guilt or selfishness, but as an authentic expression of who we are. If we do not actually do something new or different, or do the same thing with a different attitude, it indicates we have not become anything new or different from what we were.

Here's the truly wonderful thing: we don't have to worry about making any of this happen. We need only the desire to become more open and enough intention to express this desire in the simplest of prayers—*Open my eyes!*—throughout the course of any normal day. The rest we can entrust to God.

I should make it clear that the goal of openness is *not* so that we will release, receive, become, and do. They are sections of the path. The goal, and the path itself, is simply openness—that you and I might become as open as possible to our Creator, Lover, Redeemer, and Friend, to ourselves, and to other people.

Before going on to describe our contemplative path in detail, let me first tell you about another path—a very real, physical one upon which "my eyes were opened"—that represented my own first stumbling-but-deliberate steps toward openness.

In 2012, the board of directors of Sanctuary Ministries of Toronto graciously granted me a six-month sabbatical, my first ever. We say at Sanctuary that "we are becoming a healthy, welcoming community where people who are poor or excluded are particularly valued. This community is an expression of the good news embodied in Jesus Christ." Our people include many who are poor, homeless, mentally ill, addicted, or suffering the effects of sustained abuse. Such ministry is a demanding, but also profoundly satisfying, way to live.

At the time of my sabbatical, I was the executive director and had been leading the community for more than twenty years. For fifteen-plus years before that, I had been involved in outreach of one form or another among Toronto's most marginalized people.

I had identified several goals for my time away from the community and the weight of responsibility. One of those goals was spiritual retreat, and another was "research," which meant taking time to observe at some length other forms of intentional faith communities. I decided to kill the two birds with just one stone: I would visit a monastic community for purposes of research, and at the same time squeeze in a little spiritual retreat.

I settled on Quarr Abbey, a Benedictine monastery on the Isle of Wight. As an added efficiency bonus (God blesses those who multitask), the Abbey was a ferry ride across the Solent from the home of my brother Dave, with whom I would spend an additional week hiking the coast of Cornwall.

Having been intrigued by Arthur Boers's account of walking El Camino de Santiago as a pilgrim,[4] and further encouraged by his subsequent book about undertaking intentional choices and activities as a means of nurturing spiritual focus,[5] I decided to stay in the town of Ryde, about two and a half miles away, instead of in the guesthouse of the Abbey. The Rule of Benedict requires monks to offer hospitality to any who ask, and as they have been doing so since the sixth century, Benedictines are good at it!

But staying at a distance would afford me the opportunity to walk. When the body is engaged in a simple, repetitive task, the mind may be set free. It would give me time for reflection and (two birds again) make sure my legs were in shape for Cornwall. Benedictines are not bound to silence, and I had a hunger to be someplace where I didn't have to talk at all about who I am, where I come from, or what I do in my daily life.

It worked out quite well; because I neither knew nor introduced myself to anyone, I spoke hardly at all during the entire week, apart from ordering food for my meals. As an added bonus, the little cell-like room I took in a bed-and-breakfast was only steps from the ocean. My soul craves open water and the boats that sail upon it.

I quickly settled into a simple routine. After an early breakfast, I would walk to Quarr in time for Lauds and stay for Terce, wandering the grounds in between, poking around the twelfth-century ruins and having lunch at the little teahouse on the Abbey grounds before Sext and None, after which I would walk back to Ryde to rest, read, and wander the town. I'd have supper in a local pub before hiking off to Quarr again for Vespers and Compline, which concludes the monkish day, then return to Ryde once more, strolling through the hedgerows and the dying light.

My own spiritual heritage is largely Protestant and evangelical, so listening to monks sing their prayers and the Psalms, often in Gregorian chant, was a new, mysterious, and lovely experience. I read the Rule of Benedict and watched the monks come and go, fulfilling their spiritual office to pray seven times daily, while working at the business and maintenance of the Abbey in between. It was moving, inspiring, to see their disciplined devotion.

I admit I made it to Vigils, at 5:30 a.m., only once. Their simple, rigorous routine had to be either transcendent or anachronistic when set against the frantic, garish fabric of the "real" world. I ruminated on what it would be like to live in such a community—beautiful, and demanding, and certainly not for me!—and tried to listen for the voice of God in my own soul.

And I walked: about ten miles per day, plus my perambulations around the Abbey grounds, through the narrow and winding streets of the town, along the waterfront promenade, down dirt lanes, and between the rusted wire fencing of sheep pastures. Along a paved path, bordered by hedges and trees that created a green tunnel separating two fairways of a golf course. When the tide was out, I hiked along the beach where the wet sand gleamed and rolled like the oiled hide of some vast, somnolent beast. The watery sun struck sparks off a slate sea, and rain pecked fretfully at its surface.

Each day before leaving my little room—a narrow bed, a chair, a window with an excellent view of the neighbor's roof—I read the day's Scripture passages as provided by a lectionary. I first arrived in Ryde in late afternoon. My readings the next morning, before setting out for Quarr, included Psalm 119:18: "Open my eyes, that I may behold wondrous things out of your law" (ESV).

I was delighted. This, I was sure, needed to be my prayer for the week. This was what I wanted—to see things, deep things, in new ways. I was eager for fresh revelation. And so I stowed a couple of pieces of fruit, a bottle of water, and my Bible in my small backpack and began, map in hand, the trek to Quarr.

—————

Finding my way there for the first time proved a little more complicated than I had expected. For one long stretch, I ended up slogging along the narrow verge of a wide road while cars and trucks whistled past. My mantra—"Open my eyes, open my eyes, open my eyes"—fled when I missed a turn, struggled to interpret the instructions offered in a broad accent by a kind city worker, and had to backtrack about half a mile.

The singing of the monks restored me somewhat, and lunch at the teahouse more so. The time between prayers afforded me the opportunity to look more closely at the map, to plan a few different variations of a path that would take me along dirt roads and narrow streets and beside the ocean instead of the highway.

Every day for almost a week, I walked the path between my room in Ryde and the Abbey four times. Old houses on winding streets, hedgerows, the moss-covered seawall, the smoky early-morning sky, the ocean displaying two or three distinctly different personalities every day. The cry of gulls, terns flitting, gannets wading, a heron or crane of some kind cruising low, parallel to the water, and diving. I passed by gardens enclosed by rough stone walls, greenery and flowers spilling over, their diverse scents perfuming the air.

I stopped to pray in a small church, dating to the Norman era, guarded by tilting gravestones rendered illegible by time and the elements. No large sign announced the wonder of its great age, as would have been the case at home, had we any buildings at all so venerable. Just inside, a simple typed notice in a chipped 8½" x 11" frame encouraged visitors to consider the faithfulness of congregants who had faced the Black Plague, the War of the Roses, the Spanish Armada, Napoleon, and two world wars among innumerable other challenges.

Perhaps my favorite part of the path, apart from the strand when the tide was out, was that long, cool tunnel through the golf course. Pale-green light filtered through the canopy of trees; the walls of hedge were dotted with little white flowers, their petals carpeting the ribbon of asphalt beneath my feet.

On the grounds of the Abbey itself are the grey stone ruins of the original Cistercian monastery, founded in 1132. After the Dissolution in 1536, the abandoned Abbey and its properties were acquired by a merchant who dismantled many of the buildings and sold the stone. The old Abbey House remains and is still in use.

There are pastures with sheep and a handful of horses between the old Abbey site and the new buildings, which are constructed of orange-red brick in a radically different Byzantine, Moorish style. The setting is the very definition of bucolic, the archetype of English town and country.

Open my eyes.

I was certainly seeing much and enjoying it. The liturgy of the monks afforded me a kind of pleasant stasis, a suspension of the concerns and distractions that normally crowd my mind. I felt as though I was communing with God and my own soul, to some degree, but I didn't believe I was *seeing* what I was supposed to see. No revelation, nothing wondrous.

While one part of me was reveling in both the restfulness and extravagance of the experience (I had only been to England once before), another part was growing frustrated as day followed day, and I traversed the path over and over with eyes wide-open, chanting "Open my eyes!" under my breath—and nothing even remotely numinous appeared.

Trudge, trudge, trudge. Pray, pray, pray. Listen to monks. Trudge and pray some more. Listen to monks again. Read some Scripture, get something to eat. Trudge, pray, listen to monks. Repeat . . .

Nothing.

By the morning of my last full day on the Isle of Wight, *Open my eyes!* had acquired a subtext, addressed to God, that went something like this: "Look, I've worked hard for a long time—decades, in fact—and now I've taken this time off just to do this, just to see whatever it is you want me to see, and I've spent a lot of money and flown across the ocean and it sure seemed like you 'gave' me that particular saying in the very first reading of my very first day here, and I'm staying in this cruddy little room, walking a dozen miles a day, and staying away from people, mostly, so that I can really pay attention, and my time is almost up, so can't you throw me a bone here? C'mon. *Open my eyes!*"

My humble request had devolved into a crabby demand.

I had almost reached the Abbey on my second trip of the day. It was late afternoon, there was a light breeze, and the sun had made a rare appearance. I was walking along a dirt road between two pastures on the Abbey property when a handful of white dots fluttered across my vision, just inches in front of my face. Startled, I stopped and looked at what had landed at my feet. Flower petals.

Huh. Nothing special there . . . They were the same petals that carpeted the path through the golf course. Now that I thought of it, and looked a little closer, I realized these same small white flowers grew up along every fence line and were interwoven with every hedgerow I had passed all weeklong. I must have trod on or passed—how many? Tens of thousands, hundreds of thousands, surely. Millions, maybe. I bent over and, for the first time, truly saw them.

Each and every petal was the shape of a perfect, white heart.

A Prayer for Openness

Lord, open me to release, that I may receive, become, and do . . .

- *Open my eyes, that I may release what I have seen, and so see you, see myself through your eyes, and truly see others.*

- *Open my ears, that I may release what I have heard, and so hear you, become a listener, and truly hear others.*

- *Open my nostrils, that I may release what I have inhaled, and so breathe in your fragrance, be delighted by it, and breathe your Spirit upon others.*

- *Open my mouth, that I may release what I have tasted, and so taste your goodness, be made strong by the sustenance you give, and share your sustaining grace with others.*

- *Open my hands, that I may release what I have held, and so hold what you give me, be molded by your touch, and reach out to others.*

- *Open my mind, that I may release what I have understood, and so understand you, understand myself, and understand others.*

- *Open my heart, that I may release what I have loved, and so receive your love for me, love you more deeply, and truly love others.*

This prayer will serve as a kind of map as we find our way along the contemplative path of openness. Don't panic: just as having a road map handy means you don't have to memorize the entire route on a driving trip, this prayer-map is something you can return to, if necessary, when you want to move a little further along. You don't have to memorize the prayer. All you need to know is what part of the path you are traveling along today.

Five senses, plus mind and heart: seven legs of the journey.

Almost any path between two points can follow a variety of courses. The butcher shop in my neighborhood is only two blocks away from my front door by the most direct route, but if, instead of turning left at the café, I continue south, I can walk all the way to the shore of Lake Ontario. Sometimes I do that, then walk along the beach for a half mile or so (the water sparkling, the dog roaming happily around) before turning north again, up across the Boardwalk and through the park to Queen Street. Left again, along the busy street for several blocks, and lo—there's the butcher shop! The trip has taken me almost an hour instead of five minutes, but it's been time well spent.

Sometimes the path to the butcher shop begins when I hop on my bike in the morning and cycle off the five miles or so in the opposite direction to Sanctuary. I may spend eight or ten hours there, and even cycle to meetings in other parts of the city, before heading home—and stopping at the butcher shop on my way.

Just so, there are any number of ways to follow our contemplative path. We could take one of the twenty-eight sections each day over a period of four weeks. We could focus on one of the seven "legs" each day for a week and keep repeating that. We might pray one simple phrase over and over, as I did on the path to Quarr, until we have released or received or become or done or thought or felt whatever it is we think we were supposed to. We could follow the phrases in the order of the prayer as it's written, or hopscotch back and forth according to our particular whims and inclinations.

Sooner or later, without really trying, you'll find that you are aware in the same moment of what you are perceiving through several senses. You'll find yourself praying that God will open you in several ways at once that are interconnected.

Whatever our choices in this regard, this contemplative path is not a course to be completed and left behind. Our senses, minds, and hearts will always provide the path of communion between us and God, and we will need to return over and over to ask him to open us up. And doing so, we will surely find, will make our lives more joyful and fulfilling.

In the chapters that follow, we'll consider what exactly we are asking with each phrase of the prayer for openness. You may choose to return to a specific chapter now and then to help you remember and refocus, or you may find that it's not necessary—you might very well develop your own shades of meaning for each aspect of the openness you seek.

Over the weeks before I began writing this book, my prayer was *open my ears*—I was very much convinced that I needed to let go of what I thought I was supposed to write, so that I could receive what God had to say, internalize it, and actually begin to write it down. It may be that circumstances in our lives make us aware that we have an immediate need of openness in a particular area.

We might even be aware that, for instance, there's a particular thought we've been hanging on to that we need to let go of—perhaps because we know it's destructive, or perhaps because we're not sure what to do with it. Then our prayer might be, *Lord, open my mind, that I may release what I have understood.* We would continue to pray this way until that thought no longer dominates our thinking. Then we could move on: *Open my mind, that I may understand you . . .*

What I mean by prayer, as it applies to this contemplative path, is simply this: take one phrase—one leg or section—of the prayer for openness, and say it. Take it with you through the day, and say it whenever you think of it. Speak it aloud, mutter it, think it silently, write it down—it doesn't matter how you express it.

Before you even get out of bed in the morning, take thirty seconds for yourself. Thirty seconds. Be silent and still for the first bit. Be aware of what you see, hear, and feel. Choose your phrase and say it slowly for the first time that day. If your thirty seconds hasn't run out yet, say it again.

You can continue the contemplative prayer while you eat breakfast, take a shower, or make your way to work. You can pray—*open my heart*—while you're in the middle of a difficult conversation. While watching your child's Little League game or dance class, while shopping for groceries, while paying the bills or struggling over the family accounts, while sitting through a tedious business meeting or church service, while making dinner for yourself, alone again.

There is nothing magical in the phrases of the prayer. They're not an incantation or a mantra. You are simply declaring to God your desire to be open to him. He'll do the rest.

Do you remember the story Luke tells of the blind man begging near Jericho? As Jesus was passing by, the man kept calling out, "Jesus, Son of David, have mercy on me!" Jesus had his disciples bring the blind man to him, and he asked, "What do you want me to do for you?"

"Lord, I want to see," he replied (Luke 18:35–43).

And of course, Jesus gave him sight. But he wanted the man to identify his desire first.

So, why repeat the phrases? Very simply, to remind ourselves of our intention, and to cultivate our awareness of the millions of heart-shaped petals over which we are walking every day.

As I experienced on the path to Quarr, it's important to be patient. Sometimes the delay has its rewards—if I had noticed the first time I saw them that the petals that were everywhere were shaped like hearts, I doubt I would have understood them as an expression of God's love for me, personally. I would have just thought, *Oh, look, heart-shaped petals.* The message instead was twofold: "I love you" and "I'm communicating with you all the time, whether you notice it or not."

———

Faithfulness also matters. The more consistent we are in actually inviting God to open us up, the more attuned we will become to the many ways in which he is already communing with us.

But don't be discouraged if you start well and completely forget about the whole thing by the time you get to work. This is a spiritual exercise, and like any exercise, it takes a while to build strength. Just pick up your phrase again, anytime you think of it, and work it.

Don't be discouraged if nothing seems to happen at first. We are so used to high levels of stimulation that it can be a challenge to recognize the more subtle, patient communication that seems to be the preferred tone of the Spirit.

As I prayed, *Lord, open my ears* while preparing to write, I felt that I wasn't hearing anything much, just as I had gone days and miles on the path to Quarr without seeing. Then I realized that I needed to stop and reflect—I needed to stop and take notice of the sounds around me.

Followers of Ignatian spirituality (developed in the sixteenth century by Ignatius of Loyola, the former mercenary who experienced a radical conversion and went on to found the Society of Jesus) engage in a practice called Examen. Usually at lunch and before bed, they review the events of the day and try to identify where God has been present within them.[6]

That night I did something similar, but even simpler. *Open my ears*, I prayed again, as I lay in my bed. *Help me actually hear what you said to me today.* As I reviewed the events of my day, I discovered that God had spoken several times in very deep ways, although I hadn't recognized his voice in the moment.

One young woman had told me that her parents were splitting after many years of marriage and that it was breaking her heart. Another young woman, who lives very close to the street, described with tears how profoundly she missed two mutual friends, one who had died of an overdose and another who had been beaten to death. Then she went on to say that she loved our Sanctuary community and was convinced it had saved her life. Two homeless men in their forties, at separate times, declared they considered me to be their father—an incredible honor!—as their own had done such miserable, destructive jobs of it. A middle-aged, mentally challenged woman who had been living in a shelter to escape an abusive relationship shared with me her hopes for secure, dignified housing.

As I recalled these conversations, I realized that I had, indeed, heard God speaking. These dear people had granted me precious gifts from deep within their souls. I didn't know what it all meant—I couldn't translate from their words a direct message instructing me to do something specific—but I knew I had received something wonderful. I had been more open than I had realized, and realizing it encouraged me to become more open still. You can probably imagine some ways in which receiving helped me to release, to become, and encouraged me to do.

The bookends to a day's contemplative journey on the path of openness are *expressing our intention* to become more open at the beginning of the day, as well as throughout it, and *examining our progress* along the path at the end of it.

Remember, you may not be able to identify clear progress on any given day. It doesn't matter—it's not a race, and there is no final destination. The path *is* openness. As I discovered, you will be opening up even when you don't realize it. And there will be times when it's obvious—lying right there in front of you!—that it's happening.

Even the longest path must begin where you are standing right now.[7] Let's begin.

2

Open My Eyes

Lord, open my eyes,
that I may release what I have seen,
and so see you,
see myself through your eyes,
and truly see others.

SEEING

The healthy human eye is capable of distinguishing millions of different shades and colors. On a clear day, standing on flat ground, it can see as far as the horizon will allow—about three miles, before the curve of the earth obscures vision. On that same clear day, standing at the bow of a boat at the mouth of the Niagara River, I have often been able to discern the murky outline of the office towers of downtown Toronto twenty-eight miles away. (And I'm nearsighted.) Most people have a field of vision of almost 180 degrees—the world in front of them—without even turning their heads.[1]

Our eyes give information that helps us calculate the speed, distance, size, shape, and even the texture of objects. Think of riding in a car and watching another vehicle approaching from the opposite direction. Our eyes relay a constant stream of information that tells us how big the other car is, how fast it's traveling, its size and color, and a lot more, even though its position relative to us is changing rapidly and constantly. We calculate whether or not it's safe to make a left turn with that vehicle bearing down on us—all the while, perhaps, noticing that it's the newest model of a favorite make, although that shade of pale, metallic blue doesn't really do it justice.

Our eyes do all this by admitting light for our brains to interpret.

But our eyes do a lot more than merely relay images to our brains. They sparkle when we're happy and tear up when we're sad. The dilation of pupils is one of the many subtle signs we read in each other's eyes, helping us interpret the nuances of both verbal and nonverbal communication. Watching the direction in which a person looks while talking to us gives clues as to whether or not they are telling the truth. (Looking left, for right-handed people, is thought to indicate searching the memory banks for details. Looking right, or fluttering the eyelids, usually demonstrates deception. Eye contact usually indicates truthfulness, but too much eye contact leaves us wondering.) We may admire many aspects of an individual's physical beauty, but it's when our eyes connect that we begin to discern character.

"Eyes are the windows of the soul," says the old proverb. (The Roman orator Cicero said that the nose and ears were windows too.) Scientists agree, according to a 2007 article in *Discover* magazine. Reviewing research done at Örebro University in Sweden, the article asserted that patterns in the iris can give an indication of whether we are warm and trusting or neurotic and impulsive. The iris, these scientists pointed out, also plays a role in shaping part of the frontal lobe of the brain, which influences personality.[2]

What you see influences who you become! And, of course, each iris is so uniquely characteristic of its owner that they are increasingly being scanned to determine identity for security purposes. Nobody else has eyes just like yours.

Referencing recent psychological research, Richard Rohr wrote that "infants see themselves entirely mirrored in their parents' eyes, especially the mother's. What her eyes tell us about ourselves, we believe and become."[3] He went on to describe prayer as "receiving and returning the divine gaze." The apostle Paul connects our eyes with our emotions and intellect in one of his prayers for the Ephesian people: "I pray that the eyes of your heart may be enlightened in order that you may know the hope to which he has called you" (Eph. 1:18).

The Genesis story tells us that the immediate effect of eating the forbidden fruit was that the eyes of Adam and Eve were opened to know good and evil. Seeing things the way they really are can be dangerous, apparently. And yet, the acquisition of this dangerous new sight was the means by which God's ultimate plan of redemption would unfold. Adam and Eve lost an old way of seeing and gained a new, more comprehensive field of vision.

"I see," we sometimes say when comprehension dawns.

"See you later" means "I know we'll meet up again soon"; when we do, we'll seek out our friend's eyes for the clearest indication of how he or she is doing. Even people who are blind use these expressions.

We shoot daggers with our eyes at people who have harmed us and gaze fondly on the ones we love. We stare at things we are trying to figure out or off into space when lost in thought. With a deeper, clearer understanding, we gain a new perspective—we see things differently. Any leader worth his or her salt must be able to cast a vision for the ones who follow. A favorable situation looks good, and a difficult one looks bad.

"The eye is the lamp of the body," Jesus said. "So, if your eye is healthy, your whole body will be full of light, but if your eye is bad, your whole body will be full of darkness" (Matt. 6:22–23 ESV).

Clearly, our sense of sight profoundly influences everything we say and do. It's a primary shaper of our perceptions. Our spiritual eyes, no less than our physical ones, register reality by admitting light—God's light. No wonder, then, that we pray,

Lord, open my eyes,
that I may release what I have seen,
and so see you,
see myself through your eyes,
and truly see others.

Releasing

Lord, open my eyes,
that I may release what I have seen,
and so see you,
see myself through your eyes,
and truly see others.

I'm not much of a photographer. Snapshots of family and friends on odd occasions or holiday pics are my usual limit. Like many, though, the advent of the cell-phone camera has gotten me in the habit of recording more of these moments than I used to, since I rarely remember to bring a real camera. Apart from the people I love, my most frequent subject is sunsets.

There are no two the same, but they all fill me with wonder and a longing I cannot define. I have seen skies like blue velvet, deepening to purple, trimmed with ermine clouds, slashed with red and gold as if a divine fire were burning its way through the fabric of the cosmos. Some flame within me answered.

For what am I longing? Deeper peace, greater clarity, simplicity, healing of the scars and sorrows borne by my own soul and those of my people—I long for all of this, and much more. It is, I think, in essence a holy longing, a longing for the Holy. The mere sight of such beauty at once pierces me and confers some measure of wholeness.

But not all that we see initiates desire that could be called holy.

One of the meanings of this multifaceted little word *open*, remember, is to release, to let go of something that has been constrained or held, as a bird might be released by opening a cage. What might it mean, then, when we ask God to open us up to letting go of things we have seen? What images or perceptions have we held, consciously or unconsciously, that we might need to release? How can we release them? Is this even possible?

"If your right eye causes you to stumble," Jesus taught us in his Sermon on the Mount, "gouge it out and throw it away. It is better for you to lose one part of your body than for your whole body to be thrown into hell" (Matt. 5:29).

Jesus was quite definite that it's not only possible to let go but that it may be a question of life or death. Exaggeration such as this was a common feature of rabbinical teaching in the time of Christ. Clearly, he didn't actually mean that we should tear our eyes out if we happen to see something that induces us to act or think in a sinful way—if that were the case, we would all be stumbling around with two gaping sockets.

He was, however, teaching us that there are things we see, images we register, and perceptions we develop—*view*points, if you like— that can be destructive to our relationships with ourselves, others, and God, if we don't make a deliberate choice to identify and dismiss them.

A little later, in the same sermon, Jesus said, "How can you say to your brother, 'Let me take the speck out of your eye,' when all the time there is a plank in your own eye?" (Matt. 7:4).

We can be surprisingly determined to hang on to images we know are harmful, returning to "view" them time and again, the way our tongues seek out sores in our mouths.

Reflect on the images we register in the course of a day, a week, a month.

Think of the ones that bombard us unceasingly from virtually every form of media. The covers of the magazines that line the grocery store checkout alone launch a formidable assault, reminding us that our value as human beings is in direct proportion to some obscure matrix of our youth, beauty, wealth, power, and fame.

Feminists and a great many who are just sensible people have for years decried the womanly body image foisted upon us by clothing designers and movie studios—an image that is literally impossible to attain for the vast majority of women, and is often "womanly" only in the most abstract fashion. Alternately, they portray women as idealized units produced for consumption by men. These standards are so ridiculous that even models and actresses (or that curious subset who are famous for being famous) who are already beautiful submit themselves to surgical procedures and the installation of aftermarket body parts in order to hone their images.

The same outlets promote an image of ideal manhood that is every bit as absurd: tough, solitary, unemotional, remorseless. A steely squint, two days' stubble, and six-pack abs. Set to win—to dominate—at all costs.

Such images are easy targets. We know they're false, even silly. We know they're harmful. And yet . . . we still measure ourselves against them, and come up short in our own eyes.

And what about images that reinforce cultural stereotypes, encouraging us to diminish others because of their ethnicity, gender, sexuality, religion, economic status, politics, or even body weight or the cars they drive? How do you feel when you see a homeless person or a group of young men in hoodies walking toward you on a lonely street? What does the way they look mean to you, and how have you learned to think of them that way?

Or how about pornography, a massive, worldwide industry that trades in images that are destructive to both the viewed and the viewer? Astonishing numbers of men admit to an addiction to these diabolical representations of what should rightly be a holy act. Even licit media images are rife with sexualized content. It was exactly this—the desire to have sex with someone who is another's spouse, cultivated by a kind of predatory gazing at the subject of desire—that prompted Jesus' exhortation to pluck out an eye.

These images linger, even when we think we have shoved them aside. They leave a dark residue in the mind and influence the way we look at the world around us. They are powerful in their ubiquity and may become so deeply rooted that they are very, very difficult to expel.

More difficult still are the challenges that face people who have endured or witnessed trauma—soldiers, police, firefighters, paramedics, emergency room doctors and nurses, people who have lived in war zones, adults who were abused as children, men and women who have spent time in jail or living on the street, women who have been raped, people who have endured or witnessed harassment, horrific accidents, bombings, beatings, shootings. The list goes on.

Many of my friends struggle with the aftereffects of terrible personal traumas. It's not uncommon in our community to realize that the person in front of me who minutes ago seemed quite rational, and now suddenly appears to be raving for no good reason, is in the midst of a dissociative episode: he or she is not seeing the surrounding reality, but rather a mental videotape of the terrifying event that damaged him or her in the first place. The images are more real than reality.

Now think about the perceptions all of us develop, often skewed or hypocritical, because of what we have seen. Here is where we retreat into the fortresses we build for ourselves—*I'm not like that, thank God. Those people are strange, repulsive, ludicrous, dangerous. I'm not letting anyone or anything like that get close to me again. At least I'm not as bad as . . .*

Very often, we want to help our brother with that speck in his eye as a means of pretending that the plank in our own eye isn't really there or isn't really an issue.

We are usually more eager to receive than we are to let go, but we must be prepared to release the images we have gathered and locked up inside us in order to clear space for receiving the new, life-giving sight God wants to grant us. We are stuffed full of mental pictures telling us lies about who we are. We hang on to those pictures because they're familiar and because they frame the way we see the world around us. We don't know how any of it—ourselves, our world, God, other people—will look if we let them go. We need help moving them out, and so we pray:

> Lord, open my eyes,
> *that I may release what I have seen,*
> and so see you,
> see myself through your eyes,
> and truly see others.

Receiving

> Lord, open my eyes,
> that I may release what I have seen,
> *and so see you,*
> see myself through your eyes,
> and truly see others.

What could we possibly have in mind by asking God to open us up so that we might see him? It sounds, at the very least, audacious, and possibly blasphemous. Didn't the apostle John tell us, not once but twice, that "no one has ever seen God" (John 1:18; 1 John 4:12)? He also quoted Jesus as saying, "No one has seen the Father except the one who is from God; only he has seen the Father" (John 6:46).

Of course, Jesus also taught, "Blessed are the pure in heart, for they will see God" (Matt. 5:8). But, if you're like me, this is hardly encouraging—I *know* I'm not pure in heart! And it seems unlikely that I ever shall be, in this life at least. Still, I suppose he is teaching us that it is at least possible for someone somewhere to, in some fashion, see God.

It reminds me a little of the story of Moses, grown bold with God as he grew increasingly frustrated with playing both babysitter and intercessor for the people of Israel. "Now show me your glory," he demanded as a sort of compensation. God agreed, but told him "you cannot see my face, for no one may see me and live." (Not encouraging, that.)

God placed Moses in a cleft in a rock and covered him with his hand until he had passed by. "Then I will remove my hand and you will see my back," God said, "but my face must not be seen" (Ex. 33:18–23).

All that Moses got to see was the tail of the comet that was God's glory—but the effect was so transformative that his own face became radiant and the people were afraid to come near him.

Is it possible that as our hearts and minds begin to release the many sordid, mundane, or distracting images that crowd them—as our hearts are incrementally purified—our vision for God sharpens? Is it possible that we, too, may be transformed by "seeing" him?

Still more hopeful are the words Jesus offered his disciples in the Upper Room as they celebrated the last Passover and the first Lord's Supper. With all his talk about leaving them behind and going to prepare a place for them in the Father's house (the way to which he said they knew but Thomas admitted they didn't), the disciples were confused and perhaps, like many of us, a little weary of trying to figure it all out. Philip finally said, "Lord, show us the Father and that will be enough for us."

Jesus answered, "Don't you know me, Philip, even after I have been among you such a long time? Anyone who has seen me has seen the Father" (John 14:8–9).

This *is* encouraging, because Jesus in effect was saying to the disciples that God the Father, even though he's invisible, has been in front of them the whole time—they've been looking at the Father without even realizing it. Might this be true for us too? On the other hand, the unrecognized representation of the Father is Jesus himself; so how then can you and I *see* him? Certainly not in the material sense the disciples did. We have traded one daunting task for another.

As I was making "Lord, open my eyes, *that I may see you*" my contemplative prayer for a couple of days in preparation for writing this chapter, I attended an evening event at Sanctuary. We call it our Arts Extravaganza: two consecutive evenings of music, visual art, and various performances that are the fruits of the creative souls in our little community. I entered a little late and sat on the floor with my back to the wall beside two of my First Nations (Native American) brothers. Both struggle with the destructive images of profound and repeated traumas that began in childhood and with the addictions and consequent poverty that are so often trauma's dark product.

But they are also beautiful men, and I was very much aware as I sat with them of how much they looked like the Messiah that Isaiah described: their appearance disfigured, their forms marred; despised and rejected by polite society, men of sorrows who are deeply acquainted with grief; the kind of men from whom people hide their faces, turning away from them when they sit panhandling on the street corner.[4]

A little later in the evening, I moved to a chair at the back of the auditorium. As I sat there enjoying the performances, another friend came to sit beside me. She also is street-involved, addicted to crack cocaine, and involved in the many illicit activities that fund and surround such a life. She was a little bit high and quite distraught—but also quite determined to express to me how important I am in her life. Her face shone through her tears. Her words of blessing were so extravagant it would be embarrassing to relate them here. Much later, as I lay in bed drifting off to sleep, her face, and those of the two men, continued to glow in my interior vision. In the midst of her deep pain, she had poured grace upon me. There was no doubt in my mind that the visages that floated before me in the darkness were different versions of the face of Jesus.

This is not merely fanciful. Jesus himself taught that it was so:

> Then the King will say to those on his right, "Come, you who are blessed by my Father; take your inheritance, the kingdom prepared for you since the creation of the world. For I was hungry and you gave me something to eat, I was thirsty and you gave me something to drink, I was a stranger and you invited me in, I needed clothes and you clothed me, I was sick and you looked after me, I was in prison and you came to visit me . . . Whatever you did for one of the least of these brothers and sisters of mine, you did for me." (Matt. 25:34–40)

Here is a way that I may actively choose to *see* God: by gazing unflinchingly at—by *beholding*—those in my world from whom others hide their faces. Jesus told me that when I do so, I am looking at him. (Of course, he called me to do more than look. But more on that later.)

There was another face projected on the inside of my eyelids that night. My wife, Maggie, had been away for a week, and I was missing her. She has been and continues to be a source of great healing to me and a daily channel of God's grace and love in my life. As I reviewed my day—asking, *Lord, how have I seen you today?*— there was no doubt that the memory of her face was also an image of God for me. Not an idol, but a means of his communicating to me the way he looks: loving, generous, gracious, faithful, passionate, and much, much more.

I thought, too, of a narrow slice of sky, purest blue, glimpsed earlier that day between the soaring towers of the city center. "The heavens declare the glory of God, and the sky above proclaims his handiwork" (Ps. 19:1 ESV).

These were only flickers of light on the tail of the comet of his glory, but I had seen God. "Blessed are the eyes that see what you see," Jesus said to his disciples at a point when he was overcome with joy because they were growing in faith and spiritual power (Luke 10:23). Blessed, indeed. *Thank you, Lord, for answering my prayer:*

Open my eyes,
that I may release what I have seen,
and so see you,
see myself through your eyes,
and truly see others.

Becoming

Lord, open my eyes,
that I may release what I have seen,
and so see you,
see myself through your eyes,
and truly see others.

The apostle Paul told us, "Whenever anyone turns to the Lord, the veil is taken away . . . And we all, who with unveiled faces contemplate the Lord's glory, are being transformed into his image with ever-increasing glory, which comes from the Lord, who is the Spirit" (2 Cor. 3:16, 18). Those old images that obscure our spiritual sight are removed.[5]

This is good news! The practice of gazing at God, opening our eyes to recognize the divine all around us and within us, is transformative. Medieval contemplatives called this *adoration* and often used the elements of Eucharist as a point on which to focus their attention. We can expect that even such a simple contemplative path as ours will result in us looking more and more like the One who created us—even, maybe especially, if we can't see it in ourselves. God sees it. We are changing, becoming something greater in his eyes.

The King James Version beautifully renders verse 18 this way: "And we all, with open face beholding as in a glass the glory of the Lord, are changed into the same image from glory to glory, even as by the Spirit of the Lord."

There's a big difference between seeing myself and seeing myself the way God sees me. Paul said I become a mirror of God's glory—glory building upon glory—as, with an open face, I *behold* him (hold him in my gaze) and the things that veil my sight are shredded and cast away. As we've seen, we may in this way catch the occasional, dim flicker of his glory, but what does God see when he looks in that mirror?

The human story starts out so very well. The Creator's poetry moves through stanzas of light and dark; sea, sky, and land; plants and seeds and fruit and trees and every kind of rich vegetation; the grand explosion of the cosmos; animals, fish, birds, bugs, and more, all capable of reproducing themselves. It's dramatic stuff. At the close of each stanza, the Creator steps back to consider and pronounces it good. But then the poem reaches its climax: the creation of humanity—not just one being but two: male and female, *made in God's own image*—formed to look just like him. Now, before resting, he makes a final survey of all he has made. His eye lingers on the man and woman; his great heart rises joyfully: "God saw all that he had made, and it was very good" (Gen. 1:31).

That is the very first expression in the Bible of just how God feels about you and me. He hasn't forgotten the sight.

It's a good thing, too, because, of course, the story comes off the rails very quickly. Adam and Eve blew it and were expelled from the garden, and a few generations later, dear, innocent little Humanity looks very different: "The LORD saw how great the wickedness of the human race had become on earth, and that every inclination of the thoughts of the human heart was only evil all the time. The LORD regretted that he had made human beings on the earth, and his heart was deeply troubled" (Gen. 6:5–6).

It doesn't look good. God was thinking of wiping humanity off the earth and starting over. Hold on, though.

"But Noah found favor in the eyes of the LORD" (v. 8).

Humanity had a chance after all, and it was because God was willing to look deeper, to consider the individual who was seeking him in the midst of the hordes of the uninterested. This kind of phrase is used throughout the Old Testament in an almost binary fashion: some find favor in the eyes of the Lord, and others don't; some do right in the sight of the Lord, and others don't—this is the final word on almost every king of Israel or Judah whose reign is recorded in the books of Kings and Chronicles.

It's clear that God never stops watching nations, families, individuals. Too often we hear him say throughout the law and the prophets, "my eye will not spare, nor will I have pity" on the ones who turn away from him (Ezek. 7:9). This is exactly the view I fear

God has of me. Despite all I know and believe of God as the lover of my soul, the one who pours out grace as if it cost him nothing, something in me still fears, even expects, condemnation. How about you?

This, I think, is because of our tendency to default to our own view of ourselves, instead of the view God takes.

When I look at myself, I often see the junk—especially the junk I think no one but God sees: the content of those dark closets in the dim corners of the heart's deepest recesses. One word of criticism can defeat ten words of affirmation. But when God looks at me, he sees in an entirely different manner. He doesn't turn a blind eye to my sinfulness, but he also doesn't define me by it. On the contrary, he defines me by the Image into which he is slowly transforming me. I need to learn to see myself as he does.

Does that sound like a leap? Consider this: Israel wandered in the wilderness for forty years, complaining and flirting with foreign gods all the way, because they would not trust the God who sprung them from Egypt to lead them into the promised land— but: "In a desert land [God] found [Israel], in a barren and howling waste. He shielded him and cared for him; he guarded him as the apple of his eye" (Deut. 32:10).

Or this: a man with every advantage—young, rich, powerful, educated—and who, as a result, is quite sanctimonious ("all these [laws] I have kept since I was a boy") approached Jesus seeking eternal life. Jesus knew the man was about to turn and walk away when Jesus challenged his dependence on his wealth. But, "Jesus looked at him and loved him" (Mark 10:17–23).

These and a great many other passages give me hope that God sees all of me, including the nasty bits, and still sees something lovable. It is certainly unnerving to think that "all things are naked and opened unto the eyes of him with whom we have to do" (Heb.

4:13 KJV), but then I discover that such nakedness is, to him, like that of a beloved bride to her husband.[6]

"You are precious and honored in my sight," God told his people through the prophet, "and . . . I love you" (Isa. 43:4).

Neither is this passionate, affirming, fault-defeating love generic. Jesus loved that self-involved young man specifically and personally. Likewise, John told of how Jesus fixed Peter with his gaze and gave him a new name, one he didn't then deserve, but an image of the Image he would grow into (John 1:42). According to Luke, in the midst of a hectic press of people who sought healing, Jesus stopped, lifted his eyes from the job at hand to his disciples, and, apparently speaking directly to them, pronounced them *blessed . . . blessed . . . blessed . . . blessed* (Luke 6:17–22).

God grant us the openness to have such a fearless and yet such an affirming view of how we appear in his eyes!

Lord, open my eyes,
that I may release what I have seen,
and so see you,
see myself through your eyes,
and truly see others.

Doing

Lord, open my eyes,
that I may release what I have seen,
and so see you,
see myself through your eyes,
and truly see others.

We engage in contemplation because we have a desire to change our way of being with God, ourselves, others, the world around us.

40

We want to grow, to deepen. But a change of *being* that does not change our *doing* is no change at all.

If our eyes are opened in some new or deeper manner, we can expect to see things differently than we have. Releasing, receiving, and becoming are largely about how we see ourselves in relation to the spiritual and material worlds in which we live. *Doing*, of course, is about action, moving outward; and so it is about changing the way we see others.

We will both see truly and truly see when we are fully open to the Spirit of Truth: "The world [in John's lexicon, the people and systems who turn away from God and Jesus] cannot receive [is not open to this Spirit], because it neither sees him nor knows him" (John 14:17 ESV). But to those who are open, Jesus said in announcing the imminent arrival of the Holy Spirit, "When the Spirit of truth comes, he will guide you [us] into all the truth" (John 16:13 ESV).

Much earlier, at the very beginning of his ministry, Jesus announced that this also, in part, was why he himself had come: "The Spirit of the Lord is upon me, because he has anointed me to proclaim good news to the poor. He has sent me to proclaim liberty to the captives and recovering of sight to the blind" (Luke 4:18 ESV).

Jesus has come to open our eyes so that we might truly see. The Spirit has come so that we might see truly. What, then, might it mean to see others with this kind of godly clarity?

There is a beautiful and illuminating story told by all four of the Gospel writers. This, in itself, is instructive; there are only a few stories found in all the Gospel accounts, which suggests that this one is particularly important.[7] It's the story of a (probably) poor, (certainly) excluded woman of dubious moral character who had something precious to give.

Jesus was the guest of honor at a dinner in the home of a prominent and religiously impeccable man named Simon. He and the other guests were stretched out on cushions, eating food from the platters in the center of the circle, when there was a commotion at the entrance of the house. Suddenly, the woman appeared in the dining room, trailing servants who had tried to stop her. She was well known in the town, famous for her sinful life—a person completely lacking in dignity or self-discipline, and her behavior in this moment showed it.

Her hair was shamefully uncovered and unbound; she wept loudly and her eyes were swollen and red. Lurching to a stop behind Jesus, she stood there with her head hanging, sobbing, her tears dropping onto the feet of the one she had come to see. She was clutching a jar made of alabaster and seemed utterly unconscious of the disruption she caused.

Throwing herself to the floor, she mopped frantically at the feet of Jesus with her hair—with her hair! Then she smashed the alabaster container, and scooping the pungent ointment from its shards with her fingers, she slathered those same feet. Immediately, the smell filled the house, and Simon knew the odor would linger for days.

Almost everybody present—the host, the other important guests, the disciples of Jesus—were indignant at her behavior. But not Jesus. Simon thought that Jesus was no prophet, because a prophet would see this woman was not only rude, inappropriate, and probably crazy, but also such an extravagant sinner that her very touch must be contaminating. But Jesus knew exactly who she was.

After giving Simon and the others a gentle, somewhat oblique, lesson on the connection between grace and gratitude, he said something curious: "Do you see this woman?" (Luke 7:44).

See her! How could Simon miss her? Yes, Simon was looking right at her, but Jesus wanted to know if Simon's eyes were really open: Did he see, truly see, the woman he had known, judged, and dismissed? And Jesus radically reinterpreted her rude, inappropriate, crazy, undignified, and wasteful behavior to reveal her as one who—in the midst of her neediness—loved, or perhaps worshipped, as extravagantly as she had sinned.

Imagine, now, how you might first see a person who interrupted your own dinner party, business meeting, or church service in such a manner. Perhaps, like me, your instinctive response is, "Yes, but . . ."

Mark, in his gospel, told a wonderfully enigmatic story about a blind man who was brought to Jesus to have his sight restored. Jesus was not at all offhanded about the matter: he took the man by the hand, led him outside the town, spit on the man's eyes (!), and laid his hands on him. It was an elaborate ritual.

"Do you see anything?" Jesus asked him. How was that? Did it work? Jesus never, in any other healing miracle, asked such a question.

The man's response was hesitant. Perhaps he didn't want to appear ungrateful: "I see people; they look like trees walking around."

Oh, that. Jesus put his hands on the man's eyes—I imagine him finding the hidden fine-tuning control and giving it a little tweak—and the problem was resolved. Now the man could see perfectly (Mark 8:22–25).

Perhaps your vision and mine require similar adjustment. *Every person we lay eyes on has been made in the image of God!* How challenging it is to see others this way! I am of a naturally dismissive temperament. I am perfectly capable of categorizing and judging complete strangers at a glance. To help correct this, as I ride my bike through the city I sometimes repeat to myself each time I look at someone passing by: *Made in the Image.* It helps me remember what and whom I'm really looking at. It helps defuse judgment, lust, and envy.

In the section above on *receiving*, we noticed that Jesus taught us to see him when we feed the hungry, give drink to the thirsty, welcome the stranger, and so on. As that story goes on, the people who had done all this and were being welcomed into the King's kingdom asked, "Lord, when did we see you hungry, and feed you, or thirsty and give you something to drink? When did we see you a stranger and invite you in?" (Matt. 25:37–38).

These people, whom the King pronounced *blessed* because of their actions, weren't looking for God when they engaged in these altruistic acts. They saw instead poor, needy, degraded, sick, and imprisoned men and women—people nobody else wanted to embrace. And, with eyes God had opened, they recognized their merely human brothers and sisters. Sight that has been tuned by God sees beauty in all humanity, but especially in the ones many would regard as unsightly.

God grant us such acuity of vision.

Lord, open my eyes,
that I may release what I have seen,
and so see you,
see myself through your eyes,
and truly see others.

Remember . . .

- *Be patient with yourself and with the process.*
- *What you see influences who you become!*
- *Seek to have your eyes opened, rather than seeking revelation.*
- *If you forget to ask, Lord, open my eyes, or if you get distracted, don't be discouraged. Just ask again as soon as you remember.*

- *At day's end, reflect on how—in what ways—your eyes have been opened.*

For Examen (reflection or discussion)

- *Is there a dominant image or set of images in your experience that prevent you from seeing truly?*

- *Can you remember the last time you saw something or someone that made you think God was revealing himself to you?*

- *Are there differences you can identify between the way you know God sees you and the way you see yourself? Can you imagine what you would look like if God's image was fulfilled in you?*

- *Mother Teresa used to say, when she ministered to poor and dying people in Calcutta, that she was caring for Jesus "in distressing disguise." Have you been able to recognize the face of God in someone recently?*

3

Open My Ears

Lord, open my ears,
that I may release what I have heard,
and so hear you,
become a listener,
and truly hear others.

HEARING

Have you ever seen a child, an infant barely able to stand on her own, dance to the sound of music? I'm sure you have: her eyes wide and brilliant, the little swaddled bum bouncing up and down, splayed fingers waving at the ends of outstretched chubby arms, reaching for something joyous and not quite reachable, laughter burbling from a face aglow with happiness. That child didn't need to be taught to dance. The sound she heard reached straight down into her innocent soul and set her body in motion.

The same child might be frightened into tears at the sound of a stranger's sneeze.

A couple, grown used to each other through many years of banal, daily living, hear an old song on the car radio and turn to each other with warm and knowing smiles, reliving the same cherished memory without a word.

You hear from a passing acquaintance a tidbit of "information" about someone you have known and respected for years as a person of inviolate integrity; suddenly you find yourself doubting his character.

A long-fractured relationship is brought to reconciliation by hearing a simple word of confession or apology or forgiveness. The healing process can finally begin: the balm of peace is spread on the old and festering wound.

Such is the power of what we hear.

Of all the human senses, our hearing has the greatest sensitivity and dynamic range. We register sound by processing variations of pressure in the air around us. Those tiny pressure changes are gathered by the shell of the outer ear and funneled down the auditory canal to vibrate the tympanic membrane—what most of us call the eardrum, which is a good name, since it works in much the same way as a drum.

Behind the eardrum, in the middle ear, are three bones called ossicles that amplify and transfer sound onward to the cochlea in the inner ear. The cochlea is a tiny nest of fluid-filled tubes and hairlike transmitters; these translate the vibrations into nerve impulses and deliver them to the brain, where they are interpreted with astonishingly fine discrimination as a wide spectrum of sound.

Apart from the outer ear—which, alas, can sometimes be disconcertingly large, despite its being the least important piece of our auditory equipment—the whole construction is incredibly tiny. Those ossicles, sometimes called the stirrup, hammer, and anvil (because of their resemblance in shape to a blacksmith's massive tools), are the smallest and most delicate bones in the human body.

Amazingly, with this flimsy equipment, a healthy human ear is sensitive enough to discern minute changes in atmospheric pressure.[1] Some scientists say that the level of performance of a normal human ear can't reasonably be expected from the materials involved. In other words, just how we can so effectively distinguish different levels and qualities of sound is still something of a mystery.

For most of us, understanding the mechanics of hearing isn't all that important. *What* we hear is, though, and so is how we hear it: the nature of the sound we hear, the context in which we hear it (including our own mental/emotional state, and who or what produces the sound), the message we interpret therein, and the effect it has. Sometimes music makes us want to dance, and sometimes it makes us want to smash the radio.

But hearing may be a more-than-physical experience. Most of us understand that we also possess a kind of internal ear, a way of hearing words and sounds that makes no impression at all upon our incredibly sensitive eardrums. We sense that we should listen closely to this interior voice—that it may have more important things to say than the relentless, cacophonous assault of the world around us, or the echoes of other voices that clang about in our skulls during quiet moments. And yet, perhaps, this internal "sound" may also at times be heard in the external.

Thomas Merton wrote of arriving, after "sloshing through the cornfield," at his hermitage and settling in for the night as the rain drummed on the roof:

> The rain surrounded the whole cabin with its enormous virginal myth, a whole world of meaning, of secrecy, of silence, of rumor.

Think of it: all that speech pouring down, selling nothing, judging nobody, drenching the thick mulch of dead leaves, soaking the trees, filling the gullies and crannies of the wood with water, washing out the places where men have stripped the hillside! What a thing it is to sit absolutely alone, in the forest, at night, cherished by this wonderful, unintelligible, perfectly innocent speech, the most comforting speech in the world, the talk that rain makes by itself all over the ridges, and the talk of the watercourses everywhere in the hollows!

Nobody started it, nobody is going to stop it. It will talk as long as it wants, this rain. As long as it talks I am going to listen.[2]

There are moments, aren't there, when a very ordinary, familiar sound takes on the cadence of the Divine's voice? Job 26:14 (ESV) describes a number of ways God makes his power and presence known in the natural world and then says,

> Behold, these are but the outskirts of his ways,
> and how small a whisper do we hear of him!
> But the thunder of his power who can understand?

Throughout the Old Testament, God's nearly constant lament about his people is that he has been speaking to them ("Do you not know? Do you not hear? Has it not been told you from the beginning?"[3]), and that they have known he was speaking, "Yet they did not listen or incline their ear."[4]

I don't want to miss hearing that Voice, whether it whispers or thunders. Every time I've heard it before, it was loving and tender, full of blessing even when it delivered a message to bring me to my knees: challenging, refining, comforting, affirming, anchoring.

And so I pray:

Lord, open my ears,
that I may release what I have heard,
and so hear you,
become a listener,
and truly hear others.

Releasing

Lord, open my ears,
that I may release what I have heard,
and so hear you,
become a listener,
and truly hear others.

There are many sources of noise that will obscure our ability to truly hear God and other people, but they all come from just two directions: from within and from without.

The interior noises often absorb us in ourselves, whispering of our fears, grievances, insecurities, hopes, longings, and sources of pride. The exterior noises mostly distract us, throwing up a clamor of who we should be, what we should possess, and how we should look, as well as the thrill of crisis and the escapism of entertainment.

Biblical scholar Kenneth E. Bailey told of trying to be silent in the presence of God, in the kind of context in which most of us normally live our lives. "Recently I sat in the departure lounge of an international airport inundated with words," he wrote. "At one time, I could clearly hear seven cell phone conversations, two televisions, a public announcement and three departure announcements. It was the first circle of hell."[5]

Releasing the inundating background noise of our contemporary world may have gotten more complex with the advent of cell phones, constant Internet connection, and ubiquitous television monitors, but the problem is hardly new. John Donne, the preacher and metaphysical poet of the late sixteenth and early seventeenth centuries, famously remarked on his own difficulty in engaging in deep prayer: "I neglect God and his angels, for the noise of a fly, for the rattling of a coach, for the whining of a door."[6]

Hundreds of years earlier, Thomas à Kempis urged the one who desires to imitate Christ to "fly the tumultuousness of the world as much as thou canst; for the talk of worldly affairs is a great hindrance, although they be discoursed of with sincere intention; for we are quickly defiled, and enthralled with vanity."[7]

"Enthralled with vanity"—what a spot-on description of the challenge we face with the whirling storm of sound we move through every day! We actually sit and watch TV ads, not to mention programs with the intellectual/emotional nutritional content of cotton candy. Rarely do we receive a phone call, text, e-mail message, or Facebook update that is really urgent, but we are as programmed to respond to the prompts of the devices that are supposed to serve us as Pavlov's dogs were to the bell announcing mealtime.

It's good advice to "fly the tumultuousness of the world"; advice rooted, in fact, in the practice of Jesus himself, who withdrew often from his disciples and the crowd to be alone with his Father. But most of us do not have this opportunity, or at least not nearly often enough. And the purpose of this particular path is to open us up to deeper spiritual reality in the course of our normal, daily lives— lives that of necessity are lived in the very midst of the tumult.

Furthermore, there is much that we *must* respond to at some point; and we would likely agree that while too much talk of worldly affairs might be a hindrance, ignorance of them is not much of a virtue. Unawareness simply cuts us off from the life around us.

When we pray for openness in this regard, that we may release what we have heard, we are not asking God to close our ears to the noises of the world around us. We are not asking him to shut out what people, events, or other influences have to say to us. We are asking him to help us to let go of those sounds, to avoid being swamped by them. We are asking him to help us surf or swim in the waves of sound rather than be overwhelmed by them. And we are asking him to help us not fill ourselves up with distracting noises we could easily avoid.

The sinful action of Adam and Eve wasn't the result of not listening to God, but of not releasing the other voices that spoke to them: the Serpent to Eve, and Eve to Adam. The consequences, of course, were dire:

> *Because you have listened to the voice of your wife*
> *and have eaten of the tree*
> *of which I commanded you,*
> *"You shall not eat of it,"*
> *cursed is the ground because of you;*
> *in pain you shall eat of it all the days of your life.*
> (Gen. 3:17 ESV)

We experience similar pains when external noises drown out the intimate sound of the Divine Voice: a dislocation from our spiritual home or center, a rift in our relationship with the One who made us, conflict with the people we love the most.

Throughout the history of the Israelites, each time they began to listen to other voices—foreign gods, false prophets, exotic value systems—they lost their sense of direction. Listening, for example, to the frightened gabble of the ten spies who claimed that the promised land was full of nasty giants drowned out the much quieter testimony of Caleb and Joshua. As a result, the Israelites spent another forty years wandering the wilderness.

As powerful as these external noises may seem, we cling even more avidly to the sounds within us.

Often this internal recording is on a loop, replaying over and over words and phrases that define and constrict us. Parents and other significant early-life influences are usually the original sources of these messages, but with time we co-opt them for ourselves, repeating them in our minds until they become ingrained in our identity: *I am worthless; I am better than others; I am entitled to [fill in the blank]; I don't deserve good things; I am God's gift to men/women; I am undesirable.* Our minds are so flexible that we may even hear and believe internal messages that are in direct conflict with each other!

We, each of us, are the suns of our own internal solar systems. We tend to see only that upon which our own light shines, and then only from our own perspectives. If external noises are tidal waves threatening to overwhelm us, our internal voices may be black holes absorbing every bit of light we produce.

Jesus, in his parable about the sower and the seed, warns that it's possible for the Divine Voice to be choked right out: "As for what was sown among thorns, this is the one who hears the word, but the cares of the world and the deceitfulness of riches choke the word, and it proves unfruitful" (Matt. 13:22 ESV).

Still, we can't—and shouldn't—simply ignore our interior voices. Nor are we able to simply dismiss them, as much as we often would like to ignore "the cares of this world." Part of their power is that they are so ingrained, and even so valued ("the deceitfulness of riches"), we rarely examine them for their validity. Releasing them opens us up to do just that.

There may be much truth in them—there are times we *should* attend to the inner voices of guilt, pride, concern, excitement, anger, or sorrow. But if they are not truthful voices, we need to recognize this and begin to understand how they affect us, as they can be ferociously destructive. It is often, however, a very complex matter to discern which messages are accurate, timely, invigorating, and which are not.

No, just like the exterior noises, our interior sound tracks must be listened to and released. We hold these sounds and voices; they do not hold us. We do not need to cling to them or allow them to cling to us. We do not always need to know, right now, which messages are true and which are false. We are able, with God's help, to release them; and so we pray:

> Lord, open my ears,
> *that I may release what I have heard,*
> and so hear you,
> become a listener,
> and truly hear others.

Receiving

> Lord, open my ears,
> that I may release what I have heard,
> *and so hear you,*
> become a listener,
> and truly hear others.

A little while ago, I had my own Merton Moment, listening to the ineffable Voice in a rainstorm at night.

The bedroom I share with Maggie is in the attic of the house. With a couple of skylights, and the ceiling only the width of a rafter away from the elements, the pizzicato of rain on the roof often feels like one of the better features of the room itself.

The rain had been playing its subtle variations on a theme for some time before I climbed into bed. As I lay back, I smiled—it seemed evident that the appropriate prayer for the moment was *Lord, open my ears.* It was a gentle, soothing rhythm. I basked, eyes half closed, drifting. Moments later, without warning, a flash of lightning glazed the skylights blue white and floodlit the darkened room. Perhaps a second after that, a crack of thunder shook the house. There had been nary a rumble before, nor did any follow.

When my heart started ticking again, I laughed. It was a good reminder that I'm prone to supplying God with a script I've written myself. If you asked me to put into words what the rain or the lightning actually said, I couldn't. You might have noticed that Merton couldn't either. *Unintelligible* is how he described what the rain has to say. In fact, he wrote elsewhere, "Contemplation is always beyond our own knowledge, beyond our own light, beyond systems, beyond explanations, beyond discourse, beyond dialogue, beyond our own self."[8]

He also wrote that "it is impossible for one man to teach another 'how to become a contemplative.' One might as well write a book: 'how to be an angel.'"[9]

Nobody else can tell us what we will hear when our ears are opened to the voice of God. Nobody else can interpret it for us. We may not be able to interpret it—in words—even for ourselves. This Voice invites intimacy rather than issuing directives. In such instances, we will discover that interpretation in a literal sense has become unimportant; God is not bound by words, and neither are our thoughts. There is a communication possible, here at the core of our beings, that defies definition. The quiet breathing of the Presence is freighted with more meaning than can possibly be uttered.

Words may fail, "but the Spirit himself intercedes for us through wordless groans" (Rom. 8:26).

Even when we think we have heard God clearly, the ultimate message may be one that is better sensed than comprehended—like

Ezekiel and Jeremiah, we may find that God's Word to us is to be absorbed rather than decoded.[10]

Remember the heart-shaped petals I finally noticed on the path to Quarr? The immediate message was so obvious, so simple. *I love you.* As with the lightning and thunder, it made me laugh—mostly at myself, my bustling earnestness, and my self-involved blindness.

But almost immediately after discovering the petals, I began to snipe away discontentedly. My internal monologue ran something like this: *I know this already, that you love me. This is not news to me—I've even written most of a Very Important Book about this, remember?*[11] *I've come a long way, paid a lot of money, been diligent about avoiding unnecessary conversation and distraction, and I have blisters from walking back and forth on this path every day.* "I love you"—*that's the best you can do?*

I had been expecting something new, something radical and revelatory. I felt that my investment deserved such a return. Once the message had settled a bit—once I had begun to absorb it—I could hear a very, very quiet voice (my own? God's?) deep inside me saying, *What more do you want? Is there something—anything!—you could hear that would be better?* And I began to realize that though I had long ago comprehended those three little words, I was still a long way from truly apprehending them.

A few words about the actual sound of God's voice: I know there are people who claim to hear God speak in a literal, audible way. These people, I think, are either crazier than me, or much holier. Possibly both. Either way, they make me a little nervous.

Most of us, I suspect, do not really expect to have God call an audible in the backfield of our lives. Most of us are not bold enough to say, out loud, "God told me." Even those who are so bold are probably not claiming they heard actual words pronounced by a stentorian voice from on high. When we say, or feel, that God has said something to us, we are identifying a sound-that-is-not-sound; a resonance in our spirits with the Spirit; a sense or even a conviction that something at the core of our beings is vibrating at the same frequency as our Creator—a frequency that is beyond the range of corporal human hearing.

Sometimes this note rings clear enough that we may even translate it into the impoverished medium of words: *I love you.* But such a phrase cannot really convey the reality of a carpet of white hearts, their host flowers, grown from seedlings, nurtured by sun, rain, and the rich nutrients of the soil, spreading untended over miles by timely gusts of wind, each of which are magnificent mysteries in themselves.

Unless you are an Old Testament prophet, or Muhammad, or Joseph Smith, it's unlikely you've ever even claimed to hear God utter a complex sentence, let alone a paragraph or an entire book. (At least, not in a fashion that is capable of being translated into common speech.) Few of even the great mystics of the past have claimed to hear him in this manner. On the contrary, most have admitted that they are hard-pressed to put their revelations into words. Their writings are reflections on things seen and heard that are, in themselves, literally unspeakable.

I find this encouraging. Perhaps it means that ordinary people like you and me may also dare to hear and recognize the voice of God. (May I note here that the Bible, of course, is the most reliable source from which the careful, prayerful reader may hear the voice of God? The reason we are not addressing the reading of Scripture in this little book is not that it is unimportant—far from it!—but because there have been thousands of books written already giving instruction on how the Bible may be carefully and prayerfully read or studied; and our present purpose is an accessible path of daily contemplation rather than biblical study.)

It may be that "the talk that rain makes" is as close as most of us can get to hearing an audible representation of the voice of God. For how could we expect his actual voice to be contained by mortal tones? And why should it be any surprise that the sound of wind in the trees, gulls crying, a baby laughing, a fire crackling, snow crunching beneath our feet, water lapping the shore, the offhand comment of an old pal or a complete stranger, might be imbued, at any transitory moment, with the Eternal? That clap of thunder was the best joke I'd heard in years.

Still, we long for God to speak in unequivocal terms. This is because we desire the single-note clarity of certainty and struggle with the polyphonic obscurity of doubt. Perfect clarity is, for us, here and now, unattainable. Yet living directionless, awash in a morass of confusion, is untenable. The path between them is openness. By opening up, our own souls are clarified; we begin to filter the white noise of a million random sounds and home in on one pure tone, even as the answers to our many questions remain obscure.

"All who have come before me," Jesus said, "are thieves and robbers, but the sheep have not listened to them . . . I am the good shepherd. The good shepherd lays down his life for the sheep . . . My sheep listen to my voice; I know them, and they follow me" (John 10:8, 11, 27).

With the clarity of open ears, we can distinguish between the voice of thieves, come to steal our very selves, and the voice of the Shepherd. Sheep do not understand the words the shepherd uses—except, perhaps, a very few and simple—but they recognize the sound of *the* voice. And they know that this voice is leading them to every good thing.

God, it seems, is not in the business of giving answers. He is in the business of giving himself. And so we pray:

Lord, open my ears,
that I may release what I have heard,
and so hear you,
become a listener,
and truly hear others.

Becoming

Lord, open my ears,
that I may release what I have heard,
and so hear you,
become a listener,
and truly hear others.

We want more than to just hear, now and then, an echo of the ineffable Voice—that voice whose words we may not be able to define but whose very tone is life. We want to live daily in the rhythm of it, to have our hearing sharpened, our sinews and muscles strengthened and made limber by moving constantly to its song.

We want to become listeners, people whose very lives are characterized by an open attentiveness, tuned to hear the pure tone of the Creator that is the tonic note of every chord in creation.

"Whoever has ears to hear, let him hear," Jesus said repeatedly in the Gospels and the Revelation. Being able to hear doesn't mean we will listen. Having heard once does not mean we will listen again. The Pentateuch and the Prophets are full of God's complaint that the people have heard from him at great length, but only listen when it suits them.

"Truly, truly, I say to you, whoever hears my word and believes him who sent me has eternal life. He does not come into judgment, but has passed from death to life" (John 5:24).

With these powerful words, Jesus pointed out that hearing him and trusting the sound of his voice *are* life in its very essence: eternal life. Some of us have tended to view this teaching transactionally: we believe, and as a reward, he makes sure we'll live forever. While this may be so, there is something even deeper here. The construction of the phrase in the original Greek could be better rendered like this: "He that is a hearer of my word, and a believer on him who sent me . . ."

Jesus was describing one who is characterized by listening and believing, one whose life habit is to listen with his or her very being and to trust constantly the nature—what we have called the *tone*—of the *word* of Jesus. (If he had meant only believing the specific tenets of his teaching, he would have said *words*.) The life of the person who listens thus is *already* imbued with the nature of the Eternal, and is becoming more so. The word he or she constantly listens for is not a critical, condemning one, but a word of life so powerful it is setting him or her free from the many subtle and very present bonds of death. The tense indicates: "has passed and continues to pass from death to life."

Henri Nouwen, journaling during a time of deep despair, wrote:

> You *know* that inner voice. You turn to it often. But after you have heard with clarity what you are asked to do, you start raising questions, fabricating objections, and seeking everyone else's opinion. Thus you become entangled in countless often contradictory thoughts, feelings, and ideas and lose touch with the God in you. And you end up dependent on all the people you have gathered around you.
>
> Only by attending constantly to the inner voice can you be converted to a new life of freedom and joy.[12]

Dear Henri, whose own life supplied such a poignant illustration of what it means to be a "Wounded Healer,"[13] reminds us that what moves us to become listeners to the inner voice, the One voice, is our neediness, our sinfulness. We have such a difficult time listening to God rather than to the myriad voices around us. We cannot afford to be detached from the voice that speaks healing.

The gospel of Luke describes how "great crowds gathered to hear him [Jesus] and to be healed of their infirmities" (Luke 5:15 ESV). "To hear him and to be healed"—Luke used that phrase repeatedly; there's a direct connection between our hearing and our healing.

A little further on, Luke quoted Jesus: "My mother and brothers are those who hear the word of God and do it" (Luke 8:21 ESV).

This is the healing result of becoming listeners with open ears: we find ourselves in God. We discover we belong in his family, that we have the same DNA. (*Doing* is critical, too, as we know; more on that in the next section.) The more deeply this reality sinks in, or the more deeply we sink into this reality, the more confident we become that the distinction between our own inner voice and the voice of God within us is moot.

Thomas Merton, with his usual elegance and depth, expressed it like this:

> God utters me like a word containing a partial thought of Himself.
>
> A word will never be able to comprehend the voice that utters it.
>
> But if I am true to the concept that God utters in me, if I am true to the thought of Him I was meant to embody, I shall be full of His actuality and find Him everywhere in myself, and find myself nowhere. I shall be lost in Him: that is, I shall find myself. I shall be "saved."[14]

When we ask God to open our ears to become listeners, we are asking him to heal us, to convert us "to a new life of freedom and joy." Like the story Mark told about the healing of a deaf man, we are asking him to come close enough to stick his fingers in our ears, heave a sigh, and command them to be open.[15] We long for that nearness. That lucky man! The first sound he heard was the voice of Jesus.

We are asking him to open a deep channel into our inner beings, so that we might hear there the word that gives us life, the continual melody of grace that roots us in affirmation instead of condemnation.

We are asking to become listeners who don't need to exchange the purity of the Divine tone into the miserably inadequate currency of words; to become open enough to hold what we hear without having to define it and file it away for future use; to learn, instead, to dance to the rhythm and melody of the song of the Creator.

We are asking for deliverance from the interior bedlam of our unquiet souls, and the maelstrom of the world without, into the serene chamber that is filled with the eloquence of the sound of God breathing.

We are asking that we might become lost in the sound of him—to be able to listen past our own need to speak, to justify, to complain, to pontificate, to accuse, to shout out our anger or disappointment or fear or greed, to holler, "Here I am! Listen to me!"

We are asking to find ourselves in him, to become so tuned that our inner voices and his voice within us strike the harmonics of one note. We are asking him to whisper to us things too wonderful to know.[16]

And so we pray:

Lord, open my ears,
that I may release what I have heard,
and so hear you,
become a listener,
and truly hear others.

Doing

Lord, open my ears,
that I may release what I have heard,
and so hear you,
become a listener,
and truly hear others.

When we have been asking God to help us release the many noises and competing voices of the world around us so that we can better hear him, why would we ask him to open us up to truly hearing others?

Every sound, every voice, carries within it a trace of the Voice that gives voice—the Word that was in the beginning and spoke the cosmos into existence.[17] The cosmos is still sustained by the word of his power.[18] Perhaps, then, we can trust that if God opens our ears, we may hear in the voices of others his own voice. We can hope that if we listen well, some of the people to whom we listen may begin to trust that God is listening too.

The only voice worth listening to is the divine Voice; every truth, wherever it is found—and it can be found in some measure almost everywhere, and in almost everyone—is his truth; every true expression of grace or love or mercy is, ultimately, spoken by him, regardless of the medium through which he speaks.

And yet, God himself is not only a speaker, a voice with a message to convey; he is also a listener. He heard Abel's blood crying out to him from the ground. He heard the people of Israel crying out in misery because of the oppression of their Egyptian slave masters. He hears the cry of the one whose brother oppresses him economically.[19] The psalmist cries out in every sort of human distress and is confident (mostly) that God hears him. And we are praying these prayers for openness because we believe God hears us, too, and responds.

God calls us to be holy, a call that may be daunting, since most of us feel—quite rightly—that we are anything but holy. But at its simplest, this call is an invitation to become, even very slowly, more like him: "As he who called you is holy, you also be holy in all your conduct, since it is written, 'You shall be holy, for I am holy'" (1 Peter 1:15–16 ESV).

We are asking God to help us become more like him, so that we may listen to others the way he listens. Listening as God does is a sacrificial act, and it leads us out of solitude and into community.

The sacrifice of truly listening to others is that it requires us to set aside our own agendas, preconceptions, and interpretations so that we can be fully open to what that other person has to say.

Life and career coaching is a relatively new discipline, requiring the coach to listen carefully to what the client has to say, and even to discern what the client is as yet unable to put into words. Approaches vary, but many identify three levels of listening to other people. The first, sometimes called subjective or internal listening, is what most of us engage in most of the time. At this level, studies suggest that we only retain a percentage of what we hear because we are paying closer attention to our own internal monologue than we are to the person speaking. Often, we are waiting for the speaker to be finished so that we can speak ourselves. We relate everything the speaker says to some aspect of our own experience: "You're going to New York this weekend? I was there a couple of months ago! Love the Guggenheim . . ."

At the second level—objective listening, or listening to understand—we are totally zeroed in on what the speaker is saying. Our own "stuff" does not intrude. We're collecting the facts the speaker relates to us, as well as a sense of his or her perspective, and we retain them well enough to be able to relate them back to the speaker.

Global or intuitive listening takes us to the third level. Here, we are synthesizing the speaker's actual words, body language, context, level and character of emotion, and a variety of other factors so that we understand what he or she really *means*, not just what is being said. It's not uncommon for an effective listener to understand that meaning more clearly than the speaker! It's at this level of listening that we are most open.[20]

This kind of listening can be costly. God truly hears our cries, hears the depth of their meaning with a perfect comprehension, and so understands our needs in a way we can never fully understand them ourselves. It's because he hears our cries that Jesus came, suffered, and died. That was the cost of really listening.

Listening deeply to others may sometimes mean we are able to receive from them expressions of real blessing, but at other times it may mean that our own souls are bruised by their pain. However, if we can manage to listen without making ourselves responsible for fixing the hurt—this is part of what openness allows—even this can be a redemptive experience. Doing so leads us deeper into the heart of God, who is unafraid to bear our sorrows.

A secondary but incredibly important function of the physical inner ear is to assist with our sense of balance. It tells us if we are upright or horizontal, in motion or at rest, and turning, tilting, rising, falling, and more.

In a metaphoric way, our inner spiritual ear can also provide us with some equilibrium, helping us balance our need of both solitude—where we can learn to release the noises of the outside world and listen for the quiet, intimate voice of God within—and community, where we learn to listen outward.

We are not hermits, those of us who choose to tread the path of openness. You and I are living in a real, workaday world, with and among a great many other people. Hearing others is unavoidable in that world. Listening to them with ears God has opened is impera-tive if we want to be people who are open. As Peter wrote, "No prophecy [speaking forth] of Scripture is of any private interpreta-tion" (2 Peter 1:20 KJV).

By this we understand that truly hearing the voice of God is never an exclusively individual matter. Our Western culture has elevated individualism almost to the status of a religion, often asserting the rights of the individual over the welfare of the com-munity. But God, the Triune God, is the original community; he never acts only for the individual. Listening to God always leads to listening to others.

What will we hear if we listen to others as God listens? Without interpolating our own needs, desires, interests?

It would be rash to put any restriction on the infinite range of what we *might* hear, but we will certainly, certainly find ourselves listening to the cries of people's hearts—the cries that are wrenched from them in their sorrow, affliction, need, or oppression.

God heard the cries of Hagar, thrice oppressed: enslaved, impregnated, cast out. He heard the cries of Abram and Sarai, as well as Elizabeth and Zachariah, in their barrenness; the repeated cries of his people Israel through the centuries when they were threatened by hunger or military oppressors; the cries of poets and prophets when they were struck down by an overwhelming aware-ness of their own sinfulness, powerlessness, or grief. Jesus heard the cries of the lame, the blind, the sick, the deaf, the lepers, and the bereaved. He hears, and has always heard, the cry of the lost—you and me.

To sum it up in a phrase, God listens to the poor. And he insists that we do too: "Whoever closes his ear to the cry of the poor will himself call out and not be answered" (Prov. 21:13 ESV).

Seeing and hearing are the first steps in any real enactment of kingdom justice, for they recalibrate our understanding and values—tuning us to the One who never turns his eyes or ears away from the plight of people who are oppressed, who understands perfectly not only their words but the full meaning of what he hears.

True contemplation leads inevitably to engagement; we cannot see others in their need or hear their desperate cries and remain disengaged. In such cries we will hear of situations, systems, bodies, minds, and hearts that cannot be fixed, and we will often be at a loss as to what we might do. In our busyness, even the thought of getting involved may make us quail. But we do not have to make anything happen; we will hope and pray for openness to follow whatever course of action God lays out for us.

But first, we listen. And we pray:

> Lord, open my ears,
> that I may release what I have heard,
> and so hear you,
> become a listener,
> *and truly hear others.*

Remember . . .

- *If God is speaking to you, you may not always be able to translate what he says directly into words.*

- *Sometimes, silence may also be a mode of communication.*

- *Comprehending words doesn't mean you have fully understood their import. We often need to hear the same simple message many times before we fully take it in.*

- *God is calling us to action. But first, we listen.*

- *If we only read and think about openness and do not actually make it a habit to ask God to open our ears, we are wasting our time.*

For Examen (reflection or discussion)

- *What words or phrases on your internal loop play repeatedly, defining and constricting who you may become?*
- *What might it mean to you to absorb rather than decode what God has to say to you?*
- *Have you heard something (or someone) recently that sounded like the voice of God? Was there a sense, feeling, or impression that you absorbed from it beyond the actual sounds/words?*
- *How has listening with open ears connected you today to others? Are there people or is there a person to whose cries you sense you should be listening?*

4

Open My Nostrils

Lord, open my nostrils,
that I may release what I have inhaled,
and so breathe in your fragrance,
be delighted by it,
and breathe your Spirit upon others.

INHALING

On the night of a long day through which I had been praying that God would open my nostrils, I stepped outside before going to bed. There had been high winds and a hard, pelting rain earlier. The sky was a deep, starless purple, glowing slightly to the west where the lights of the downtown core reflected off the clouds. The tops of trees, finally at rest, traced a black filigree against its soft bed. I inhaled deeply.

I have had my nose broken twice; it's not the most sensitive instrument, and just breathing freely through my nostrils can be problematic. It took a minute or two of slowing down my body until I could inhale easily through my nose alone. It took a minute or two more before I could detect the subtle smell of the night.

A waft of wet soil, faint but so rich it could almost be tasted at the back of my throat. The indefinable tang of the "inland sea" of the Great Lakes: Lake Ontario, just a half mile to the south. Different, somehow, than the many smaller lakes to our north, and earthier than the clear, astringent aroma of salt water. And drifting somewhere beneath it all, delicate, detectable only on the third or fourth long, deep sniff, the perfume of blossom petals bruised by the rain.

It was like sticking my nose in a goblet of wine.

We smell as we inhale and cannot do one without the other. We detect odors because molecules of what we are smelling enter our nostrils, binding themselves to tiny fronds called cilia, which are themselves rooted in stamp-sized patches of neurons at the top of our nasal passages. The neurons transmit a message to the brain, which is then interpreted as a very specific smell.

Pause and consider this for a moment: I could smell them because I actually inhaled tiny bits of damp earth, lake water, and whatever it is that imparts to flowers their lovely aroma. The earth, the lake, and the flowers, for a brief moment, actually entered into me.

The human nose is a very direct apparatus, but for all that directness, it is incredibly subtle. Of course, we breathe also with our mouths, but it's by inhaling through our nostrils that we are able, at the same time, to detect the odors borne upon the air that sustains us.[1]

Perhaps it is this subtlety that led to a curious development of language: the ancient Hebrews, Greeks, and Romans all employed terminology that related breathing to the spirit. In fact, our own English word *respiration* comes from the Latin root *spirare*, which means to breathe. The same root gives us that familiar word *spirit*. Properly, our word *respiration* means to breathe out; *inspire* means to breathe in—to inhale (from a Latin synonym: *inhalare*).[2]

This old word, *inspire*, became first a figure of speech, a play on words: to breathe in the animating spirit of an extraordinary person or event. That figurative meaning settled eventually into the definition we are now familiar with: to be filled with an animating, quickening, or exalting influence. For example: *I am inspired by her model of selflessness.*

Our sense of smell also has the most direct connection of any of the senses to our memories. Scientists believe that the olfactory cortex—the part of the brain immediately behind the nasal passages, which processes smell—has a direct neural link to the hippocampus, the section of the brain where long-term memories are stored.

No wonder, then, that certain aromas have the power to trigger recollections of amazing immediacy and accuracy. Research shows that we have a tendency to associate distinctive smells (baking bread) with the situations in which we first encountered them (Grandma and her warm, welcoming kitchen).[3] This connection is so strong that, in many cases, our perception of the situation determines whether or not we enjoy the particular smell. Infants, for instance, who are raised in loving families where the adults smoke cigarettes tend to enjoy the smell as they grow up, while those raised in nonsmoking families usually do not.

There is, of course, an almost infinite range of smells that don't necessarily activate any deep association with our memories but that may disgust, delight, or intrigue us. They create immediate, visceral reactions: think of the pungency of a skunk, flattened on the highway; the smell of wood smoke in the cool of an autumn night; or the delicate drift of a spice you can't quite put a name to rising from the plate in front of you. What we smell warns us—stay away from that chemical smell that sears your nostrils! or don't drink that sour milk!—or invites us: try a bite of this samosa, breathe deeply of this rosebud, and relax.

All these are borne on the air we breathe in, the air we *inspire*. As we inhale, we ingest the odors of the world around us, and without even thinking about it, we feed our bodies the oxygen that enlivens us.

Try this as you lie down to sleep: breathing slowly and deeply through your nostrils, trace the path of the air you inhale into your body. Pay attention to the feel of the air as it passes through your nasal passages, down your throat, past your heart, and into your lungs. If you're still and attentive enough, you can easily feel the air moving all the way down to about the bottom of your rib cage.

In terms of the actual physical sensation, we lose track of it from there; but we know that our lungs filter and convert the air we breathe into the elements useful to our bodies, delivering oxygen to our hearts, where it is mixed with the blood that pumps its way through every vein to every organ, every extremity, in our entire complex selves. Without oxygen, our blood is useless. Without inspiration and respiration, we die.

"The LORD God formed a man from the dust of the ground and breathed into his nostrils the breath of life, and the man became a living being" (Gen. 2:7).

Inspiring influence. The half-conscious associations of memory. Warnings and invitations. And carrying it all to the deepest places within us, we inhale the stuff of life itself, both physically and spiritually.

Is it any wonder, then, that we pray:

> *Lord, open my nostrils,*
> that I may release what I have inhaled,
> and so breathe in your fragrance,
> be delighted by it,
> and breathe your Spirit upon others.

Releasing

Lord, open my nostrils,
that I may release what I have inhaled,
and so breathe in your fragrance,
be delighted by it,
and breathe your Spirit upon others.

Every few seconds we inhale and exhale. Perhaps twenty thousand times every day, we take in the air our bodies need; our complex respiratory system sorts and filters what our nostrils have gathered, and a moment later expels the molecules that are unneeded. The vast majority of the time we're not even aware it's happening.

As we pray, *Lord, open my nostrils,* so becoming more conscious of the air we take in and the odors that are borne upon it, we are also really asking that God would make us aware of the fact that our souls, too, are continually inhaling the stuff of life and death—influences positive and negative, and cues to memories and associations that may affirm or cripple us.

We must exhale in order to inhale.

While our sense of smell can quickly tell us that something is dangerous or unpleasant, and our lungs filter out most of what we don't need from the air without conscious thought, our souls may not always be so quickly discerning. Furthermore, as the powerful aroma of manure hardly registers to a cattle farmer, so prolonged familiarity may deaden our senses to the far more subtle smells of spiritual toxins.

Just as we cannot stop breathing, so our spirits never cease taking in the influences, warnings, invitations, and deep, unconscious associations provided by our experience and environment. Our spirits cannot help but inspire the good or utterly corrupt aromas around us. We need help to do, spiritually, what our bodies usually do with such automatic ease: retain the good, and release the toxic or unnecessary.

Let's pay attention, then, to these three elements connected to spiritual inspiration and respiration: the often subconscious *associations* we make because of our own memories; *warnings* of danger or ill health that may be so subtle, or familiar, that we may easily miss them; and the *influence* of people, ideas, or values whose superficial attractiveness may cloak a negative direction.

The associations we make in daily life, because of memories that remain in our conscious minds, shape how we perceive the world around us. While it is a good thing to learn from experience, memory may be an uncertain, shifting foundation upon which to build. It may not be accurate; it is certainly highly subjective; and the impressions that move us may be powerful beyond proportion to the actual event.

Consider: "We remember the fish we ate in Egypt that cost nothing, the cucumbers, the melons, the leeks, the onions, and the garlic" (Num. 11:5 ESV).

This is what the people of Israel began to mutter when they grew bored with eating manna day after day. It's easy to imagine that as they plodded through the wilderness, they could almost smell the fish frying. The cool, delicate whiff of a cucumber, or the refreshing sweetness of a melon cut open on a blazing hot North African day. The rich, pervasive tang of leeks, onions, and garlic bubbling in the pot. (When we think of favorite foods, it's the aroma we remember first. A pot of chili, BBQ ribs, Thanksgiving dinner. Can you smell them?)

A veritable smorgasbord of food, they'd had—and free! Eating every day like kings and queens!

But of course, their memories were highly selective. The cost of that food was slavery, the deaths of their children, backs broken by the lash, and hard labor. Their lives were made bitter, the opening chapter of Exodus tells us, and the Egyptians used them ruthlessly. God himself said, "I have indeed seen the misery of my people in Egypt. I have heard them crying out because of their slave drivers" (Ex. 3:7).

It would be a recurring problem of perception for the people of Israel. The simple memory of the smell of food cooking, and its association with the immediate comfort it brought them in a time of despair, would skew their perspective. The distortion caused them not only to forget the terrible oppression from which they had been delivered, but it also blinded them from the path to freedom on which they wandered.

Forty years they spent in the wilderness as a result, and all who left Egypt as adults died before they entered the promised land. They were too stuck on an old, inaccurate memory to claim their new life. It may be the same for us.

"My wounds stink and fester because of my foolishness," wrote David in a psalm in which he used bodily weakness, illness, and injury as an extended set of metaphors to describe his sense of spiritual pain and alienation from God (Ps. 38:5 ESV). In this phrase, the awful smell that attends the putrefaction of flesh is directly associated with the psalmist's foolishness. He has thoughtlessly done damage to his soul, and even worse, he has done nothing to clean or care for the wound.

Years ago a homeless man came to see Keren, a nurse who then worked at Sanctuary. She had seen him hovering week after week outside the mobile clinic at a downtown stop. When he finally got up the courage to enter, he asked Keren for Tylenol, as his feet hurt. She insisted that she must see them before giving him any medication, and the man reluctantly took off his boots. His feet were black from frostbite, giving off the unmistakable stomach-turning odor of gangrene. Parts of both had to be amputated in order to save his life.

I wonder, are there ways in which we have foolishly allowed spiritual wounds—perhaps relatively simple and treatable, in themselves—to fester until they become infected, and that, left long enough, may threaten our very lives?

In language similar to David's, Job described his own quite different condition: "My breath is strange to my wife, and I am a stench to the children of my own mother" (Job 19:17 ESV).

Inspiration—the animating influence of others on one's own life—is not always positive. How many mass murderers in America have been "inspired" by dark figures from movies or by other murderers? There have been a shocking number of cases in which young women have been inspired to commit suicide by the seemingly empathetic counsel of online ghouls who are only too willing to discuss effective methods and more. How many people have been subtly inspired to betray marriages, lie, cheat, or seek pleasure at any cost by the example of celebrities or by the glamorous portrayal of such actions on television?

But these are, perhaps, extreme situations. On the other hand, while Job's condition of life was also very difficult—family tragedy piled on top of the loss of health and wealth—most of us can identify with it to at least some degree.

In the midst of his troubles, he had become either a pariah to be dismissed or a loser to whom one may condescend. His wife said he had bad breath, and his brothers and sisters, with typical sibling tact, told him he stank. These are not the worst things one could say: his wife (his wife!) had already told him he should "Curse God and die" (2:9). Not the worst, perhaps, but certainly painfully personal!

Job's wife, and his four friends—the ones who kept coming around to tell him why God was punishing him and how he could fix it, if he would only try—provided exactly the kind of influence we all dread when life gets difficult. If Job's breath seemed a little funky to them, their attempts to inspire him were about as fruitful as nuclear fallout.

Many of us have found ourselves in similar situations. Lying wounded on the battlefield, gasping for breath; a friend, family member, or churchgoer comes along and administers, instead of oxygen, a poison gas. Explaining where we've gone wrong; why we'd do better if we just had a little more faith; how it must be that God is trying to bring to our attention some hidden wickedness in our lives. Instead of having life breathed into us, which is an infallible indication of the activity of the Holy Spirit, we die a little more.

Forever trying to do and be right, then punishing ourselves (or others) when we fail, is the "animating influence" of the fundamentalist of any religious or political stripe. Such inspiration has not a whiff of grace, but instead the reek of death, even if it is disguised by the heavy perfume of strict religious observance or high-minded philosophy.

Job knew that. Just before the comment about having bad breath, instead of submitting to their noxious influence, he began his response to these "friends" by saying, "How long will you torment me and break me in pieces with words?" (19:2 ESV).

And a little further along in the same passionate diatribe—after having described in angry, painful detail how God had broken him down, friends and family had abandoned him, and his own body had almost expired—Job breathed out, almost defiantly, perhaps the most stirring expression of faith in all of Scripture: "I know that my Redeemer lives, and at the last he will stand upon the earth. And after my skin has been thus destroyed, yet in my flesh I shall see God" (19:25–26 ESV).

Now that is inspiration worthy of the name!

Such openness allows us to let go of the old paradigms to which we have subjected ourselves, creating the possibility of being fearlessly honest with ourselves, others, and God. Paying attention to the sick smell of wounds we have allowed to fester prepares us to reclaim our health, even if radical surgery may be required in the process. Having been released from the pernicious influences of destructive examples, crummy values, and poisonous dogma, we begin to inhale the oxygen of clear, clean, life-giving faith.

That it might be so, we pray—

Lord, open my nostrils,
that I may release what I have inhaled,
and so breathe in your fragrance,
be delighted by it,
and breathe your Spirit upon others.

Receiving

Lord, open my nostrils,
that I may release what I have inhaled,
and so breathe in your fragrance,
be delighted by it,
and breathe your Spirit upon others.

When my children were infants, and I rocked them in my arms before laying them in their beds, I could tell when they had fallen asleep by the change in the gentle puffs of breath against my neck.

My father passed away with most of his family gathered around his bed. His breathing got slower and shallower with each inhalation. We could tell his spirit had flown when his chest failed to rise, and somehow, indefinably, his whole aspect changed.

In the early morning, as we are awakening, Maggie often rests her head on my chest for a few minutes. I can feel her breath on my skin, and she can feel mine on the top of her head.

These are moments of great mystery, power, and intimacy; moments that almost define life itself.

Every exhalation is a preparation for the next breath. We can trust, as we let go of what we have previously inhaled, that God will open us up—he will expand our lung capacity, so to speak, and widen and deepen our sense of smell. He will inspire us in new ways.

Teresa of Ávila described this as the awakening of the soul. She said that God's desire is to make our souls "wholly one with Him," and that, in order to do so, he

> fills it [the soul] with fervent desire, by means so delicate that the soul itself does not understand them, nor do I think I shall succeed in describing them in such a way as to be understood, except by those who have experienced it; for these are influences so delicate and subtle that they proceed from the very depth of the heart.[4]

Praying, then, that God would open our nostrils so that we might breathe in his fragrance is a deliberate movement toward a deeper intimacy with God. As Teresa affirmed, we should not be surprised or disappointed if such an intimacy cannot be quantified or described; such an intimacy is every bit as mysterious, and even more so, than that which we have with the people we love most.

And yet, although words may fail to describe this deepening relationship—as they would to define the magic that bound me to my children as I cradled them so long ago—we may still recognize its import.

"All Scripture is God-breathed and is useful for teaching, rebuking, correcting and training in righteousness," the apostle

Paul wrote to his younger friend Timothy (2 Tim. 3:16). This, perhaps, is a good place to start if we really want to inhale the fragrance of God.

Although contemplation is an intensely personal exercise, we can't afford to let it become entirely subjective, as is increasingly the case with much of Western religion and spirituality. Although God desires to speak to me personally, he does not speak to me alone. By breathing into my life, he wants to shape me so that I might live righteously—in right relationship with other people.

We keep referring to the Bible from chapter to chapter because we trust that the Spirit (Breath) of God breathes within and through it. Paul described the usefulness of Scripture in terms that parallel the means by which a loving parent forms the character of a child. And when he said that it is "God-breathed," we understand that this is an invitation to intimate relationship with that loving Parent. Reading the Bible ought to be approached as a means of laying our heads on God's chest. In order to feel someone else breathing, we must be still, and we must be close.

In contrast, but not contradiction, to this gentle, tender image, the breath of God is also a recurring image of powerful judgment and deliverance. The poetic and prophetic books of the Bible return to such images over and over. One especially striking example is the song Moses and the Israelites sang as they gathered on the far bank of the Red Sea and reflected on the manner in which God had rescued them from the Egyptian army. It contains these lines:

In the greatness of your majesty
you threw down those who opposed you.
You unleashed your burning anger;
it consumed them like stubble.
By the blast of your nostrils

the waters piled up.
The surging waters stood up like a wall. (Ex. 15:7–8)

With apologies to Major Kilgore, the salty tang of the Red Sea lapping on the shores at their feet must surely have smelled to the Israelites like victory that day. To Kilgore, a fictional Air Cavalry commander played by actor Robert Duvall in the movie *Apocalypse Now*, the aroma of napalm in the morning meant the assertion of his own will and destruction of the enemy—a depressingly typical view of "victory." To the Israelites, the smell of salt water surely meant God's judgment of the oppressor, but most importantly, it meant deliverance from slavery and death. It meant freedom, a new life, the guarantee of God's unfailing love. A powerful blast from the nostrils of God meant, at last, after hundreds of years in exile, a home of their own.

These, surely, are ingredients of the fragrance we inhale when God breathes into our lives. For his power is always bent to the goal of deliverance, not domination, and to creation rather than destruction. When we are open to his Spirit, even the dark water of death itself becomes a door opening to resurrection, eternal life, and at last, our true home.

Such "home" as we may find here on earth is dependent upon how deeply we inhale that Spirit. Where we do find it, we can be sure that we are detecting the particular fragrance of the Breath of God.

Does your home have a particular, comfortable smell? Does it feel more like home when there are onions frying in a pan or a good bottle of wine is breathing on the table? Perhaps you are fortunate enough to have a wood-burning fireplace. Perhaps someone you love wears a particular fragrance. Maybe you know that unmistakable baby smell, or even the cheesy ripeness of teenagers' socks.

Breathe deeply, and give thanks.

Long before he blew on the waters and created a path to safety for his rescued slave people, before any book of the Bible existed, "The LORD God formed man from the dust of the ground and breathed into his nostrils the breath of life, and man became a living being" (Gen. 2:7).

I have taken the liberty of removing the article (*"the* man") from this quote, as it doesn't appear in the Hebrew. The intent of the passage seems to underline that man, as a genus, and not just Adam, whose name means "Man," not only came to life, but lives because God has imbued humanity with his own life. He is not only the Source but also the Sustainer of life. The phrase *breath of life* occurs seven times in the opening chapters of Genesis, in order to reaffirm this connection; the word *breath* is used elsewhere in the Bible dozens of times as a synonym for life.

This is about far more than the mere mechanics of our hearts continuing to tick over, our lungs expanding and contracting, our synapses firing. It's about recognizing and remaining wide open to the Breath that animates us, roots us, gives us transcendent value, meaning, and purpose. In a word, *life.*

Jesus re-enacted this Creation moment with his disciples after his resurrection: "Again Jesus said, 'Peace be with you! As the Father has sent me, I am sending you.' And with that he breathed on them and said, 'Receive the Holy Spirit'" (John 20:21–22).

In a new, similarly intimate and immediate way, Jesus imbues us with divine life. He confers on those who will follow him his own agency as the presence of God in the world. God himself, the Holy Breath, takes up residence in each human life that makes itself open to him.

Each breath we take, every fragrance we register, can be a reminder of this great promise and an opening to its limitless possibilities. This is why we pray:

Lord, open my nostrils,
that I may release what I have inhaled,
and so breathe in your fragrance,
be delighted by it,
and breathe your Spirit upon others.

Becoming

Lord, open my nostrils,
that I may release what I have inhaled,
and so breathe in your fragrance,
be delighted by it,
and breathe your Spirit upon others.

Most mornings when I am home, I prepare a simple breakfast. If it's at all possible, Maggie and I sit together, munching and talking quietly, and usually we read a psalm and a passage from one of the Gospels. It's a pleasant moment of joyful calmness, a lovely foundation for the day.

But before we sit down, I make myself a long, double espresso. The making of it is something of a ritual. I clean the machine, fill the basket, tamp the grounds, lock the strainer into place, place the cup carefully. Having repeated the same actions a great many times, my movements have become concise, unhurried, and almost automatic. I look forward to the wonderful, rich smell of the coffee when the lid comes off the container. When the twin spouts begin expressing the foamy jets into the cup, beginning dark and growing paler, the aroma changes somehow: the same in essence, but more mature, like the face of a child you grew up with and encounter again as an adult.

I turn off the machine and carry the little cup and saucer to the counter, where Maggie and I will perch side by side on high stools. And before I begin sipping the espresso, I inhale deeply. I love the fragrance. It has changed yet again; now it is complete; it has become what it is supposed to be. It's a holy moment—that quiet sniff.

I'm only partly joking about it being a holy moment. And you can decry my fondness for coffee as an addiction if you like, or say that my sense of the holy must be very shallow indeed. I won't argue on either count.

But for me—although you'd never know it if you stood in the corner of the kitchen and watched, unless perhaps you caught and correctly interpreted the few seconds when my nose is over the cup and my eyes close—the entire ritual is very much like the observance of a sacrament.

It's not just that I enjoy or even need the coffee as a drink. The most potent moments are those in which I inhale their aromas. Each deliberate *inspiration* reminds me that God is present, and that he is, moment by moment, breathing the breath of life into me. The fragrance and the reminder, the deliberate awareness, mingle together and become a simple, quiet, but very real daily experience of delight in my relationship with the One who made me.

Of course, this is because I have consciously invested the making of a cup of espresso with spiritual meaning. You might do the same with frying an egg or taking a shower. But this is precisely what our contemplative path is about: choosing simple disciplines to make ourselves increasingly open to the Divine.

And I am convinced that the Divine wants to open us up to delight.

Perhaps we are so easily distracted and captivated by the many pleasures around us that seem to have little spiritual value, or may even be damaging to our souls, because we don't see the pursuit of a deeper spiritual life as something to be enjoyed. Most of our world is inclined to view the "holy" person as one who is removed from reality, either by a clench-jawed piety or the pursuit of an ecstatic experience that seems to have no rational foundation.

The English and Scottish ministers who wrote the Westminster Shorter Catechism in the 1640s knew better. With admirable brevity, they identified the key question for people who seek after God, and then answered it:

"What is the chief end [purpose] of man? Man's chief end is to glorify God and to *enjoy him forever.*"

Does the idea of delighting in God seem strange to you? As we pray, *Lord, open our nostrils, that we may be delighted by your fragrance,* may each pleasant aroma be a gift, a reminder of God's desire for us to delight in him, as he delights in us. Because he does, you know.

After the waters of the Flood had abated, and Noah and his family left the ark, Noah took some animals and birds and sacrificed them as a burnt offering: "The LORD smelled the pleasing aroma and said in his heart: 'Never again will I curse the ground because of humans, even though every inclination of the human heart is evil from childhood. And never again will I destroy all living creatures, as I have done'" (Gen. 8:21).

Well, who doesn't like the smell of BBQ? Noah and his family likely ate from the burnt offerings themselves, as did the Levitical priests later on.

Throughout the books of Exodus, Leviticus, and Numbers, the phrase "an aroma pleasing to the Lord" is the invariable tagline to each description of the burnt offerings commanded in the Law—animal and fowl flesh, and various concoctions of flour, grains, and olive oil. Breads, in other words. God didn't eat those burnt offerings, of course, but it wasn't merely the obedience of the people in making them that gave him pleasure—it was the smell! The next time you walk into a bakery and feel as if you're gaining pounds just from the aroma, remember that your enjoyment of it is a mark of your Maker on your being.

To underscore God's delight in the sense of smell, there is

another kind of offering carefully detailed in the law: incense. The incense and oils used to anoint priests and temple furniture were to be carefully blended by a perfumer according to specific recipes. One lists liquid myrrh, cinnamon, fragrant cane, and cassia blended into olive oil. God wanted his priests to come before him smelling good. Most often, in the instructions about its use, incense is described as "fragrant incense." I think the reason the word *fragrant* is repeated so often is because God wanted his people to remember: *This is not a magic potion; you're using this stuff because it smells good.*

There is a sheer, extravagant delight in pleasing odors—a delight that is mirrored in a different context in Solomon's Song of Songs. This powerful love song is redolent with sensual expression; the king, besotted with the Shulamite girl, tries to give expression to his attraction:

> *How beautiful is your love, my sister, my bride!*
> *How much better is your love than wine,*
> *and the fragrance of your oils than any spice!*
> *Your lips drip nectar, my bride;*
> *honey and milk are under your tongue;*
> *the fragrance of your garments is like the fragrance of*
> *Lebanon.* (4:10–11 ESV)

Solomon's bride is similarly enamored:

> *Who is this coming up from the wilderness*
> *like a column of smoke,*
> *perfumed with myrrh and incense*
> *made from all the spices of the merchant?* (3:6)

The king and shepherd girl describe each other, and their emotional and sexual passion, in eloquent, intimate terms—and over and over, they use the language of perfumes, fragrances, spices, the aromas of fruit and wine to express the thrill of being joined together.

Most commentators, dating back to the ancient Talmudic scholars, believe that the Song is about more than the romantic relationship of two historical people. The old rabbis taught that it was the highest, holiest expression in all Scripture of God's passion for his people, and of the passion they ought to have for him.

Intimate love between two people, the aroma of good food cooking, the "nose" of a glass of wine, a carefully blended perfume, a bouquet of roses, the smell of the sea or pine sap or baking bread or rich earth freshly soaked with rain or coffee brewing: all these can be simple reminders of the eternal invitation to open ourselves to the delight found, ultimately, in God.

We pray with David the psalmist, "May my prayer be set before you like incense; may the lifting up of my hands be like the evening sacrifice" (Ps. 141:2).

And we add:

> Lord, open my nostrils,
> that I may release what I have inhaled,
> and so breathe in your fragrance,
> *be delighted by it,*
> and breathe your Spirit upon others.

Doing

> Lord, open my nostrils,
> that I may release what I have inhaled,
> and so breathe in your fragrance,
> be delighted by it,
> *and breathe your Spirit upon others.*

Have you ever met someone whose very presence seems to confer a blessing upon others?

Many years ago now, I met Henri Nouwen for the first time. My friend Mike Clarke introduced us after Eucharist, at Daybreak, a L'Arche community north of Toronto where Henri lived. The three of us gathered in Henri's very modest bedroom—a single bed in the corner, neatly made with a colorful Latin American spread on it; a small student's desk; a couple of chairs; and a tiny coffee table.

One of Henri's many gifts was that of listening. Although he was, at times, almost desperate for others to really listen to him, he gave me the sense that morning that every word I spoke was precious to him. He sat on the edge of his chair, leaning forward and nodding, long arms and legs folded at awkward angles. I was not used to unburdening myself to someone—well, to anyone, really, but especially to someone I had met only moments earlier.

And yet, I found myself pouring out the tangled tale of my own painful spiritual and relational journeys, confiding details I had rarely spoken about to anyone else. I remember only one phrase of anything Henri had to say, and that came as Mike and I were leaving.

I was already halfway out the door, feeling a little foolish for having blabbed at such length, filling up the time we had with my own nonsense and wasting the opportunity to hear from this wonderful spiritual writer and thinker.

"Let me bless you," Henri said.

I didn't know what he meant, but I turned back to him. Henri embraced me gently, his hands splayed lightly on my shoulder blades. I could feel his breath on my forehead. Separating himself by a half step, one hand on my shoulder, with the thumb of his right hand he made the sign of the cross on my forehead.

I am not Roman Catholic. Where I grew up, Catholics—especially priests—were highly suspect. Although I had often been prayed for, nobody had ever blessed me, nor made the sign of the cross on my forehead. If you had asked me thirty seconds earlier, I would have said that such things—embracing, breathing, blessing, making ritual motions—were mumbo jumbo.

Even more than Henri, his longtime partner in ministry and literary executrix, Sister Sue Mosteller, is the kind of person who radiates the presence of God. I bumped into her on the street, in my own neighborhood, a little while ago. She was in a hurry, on her way to visit a friend. We had only a few moments to speak, and neither of us said anything even remotely profound. And yet, I walked away feeling that the Holy Spirit had breathed on me. Sue would laugh and shake her head at that.

I would dearly love to be that kind of presence in the lives of others.

If, like me, your instinctive response to the very idea that you could be such a presence is *Fat chance!* and an inward snicker, there is good news. Consider these words of the apostle Paul, written to the church in Corinth—as dysfunctional, fractious, prideful, materialistic, licentious, and skeptical a group as you'd be likely to find anywhere:

> Thanks be to God, who in Christ always leads us in a triumphal procession, and through us spreads the fragrance of the knowledge of him everywhere. For we are the aroma of Christ to God among those who are being saved and among those who are perishing, to one a fragrance from death to death, to the other a fragrance from life to life. Who is sufficient for these things? (2 Cor. 2:14–16 ESV)

It takes real faith to believe that we are the aroma of Christ, spreading the fragrance of the knowledge of him to people all around us. I'm glad Paul included that last phrase. Who is sufficient for these things? Not me!

We can't breathe this kind of life into the lives of others by trying hard. The assumption of a sanctimonious demeanor won't do it. A great education, high moral standards, exemplary personal grooming habits, or being able to quote reams of Scripture might not help either.

Because, thankfully, it's not about us. It's about Christ.

When Paul wrote that we are the aroma of Christ, he meant that we are like the smell of those Old Testament offerings that God enjoyed so much. Christ is the sacrifice, and we are the fragrance that rises from the sacrifice to the nostrils of God. This fragrance spreads to others, too, just as the smell of the sacrifices wafted through the camp of the Israelites. This is accomplished not by us doing anything, but simply by being people in whom Christ is present.

Those who are being saved—people who have laid their hearts open so that the Holy Spirit can take up residence there—recognize this fragrance as a life-giving breath, a waft of divine perfume. But those who are closed to that Presence—*perishing*—can smell only death, death to their worldview and their personal autonomy.

We pray that God will open us up to breathe his Spirit upon others because this fragrance of life can only come from him, the Source of life. We can't create it, summon it, or control it. We're not sufficient for these things.

Remember the story of poor Mary, the abject, bawling party-crasher whom Jesus encouraged Simon to truly see? The biblical accounts don't tell us what Simon's ultimate response was, although the naming of him perhaps indicates he eventually became a follower of Jesus. We do know that it would have been many days before he would be able to forget about that sinful woman's act of devotion: "Then Mary took about a pint of pure nard, an expensive perfume; she poured it on Jesus' feet and wiped his feet with her hair. And the house was filled with the fragrance of the perfume" (John 12:3).

In all likelihood, Mary had no intention of breathing out the Spirit on Simon. She was focused on Jesus. But the fragrance of her worship lingered in Simon's house for a long time. Usually formulated as a thick and intensely aromatic, long-lasting essential oil, nard was one of the ingredients used by Levite priests in the sacrifice of incense, and was also commonly used to anoint bodies for burial.

For weeks afterward Simon must have thought about what Mary had done, and what Jesus had said about it, each time he came and went from his house. That perfume had been intended for Jesus' death, but I like to think that Simon came to the point of understanding his own need for forgiveness, inhaling it deeply as the fragrance of life. Whatever the effect in Simon's life, it was the by-product of Mary's devotion to Jesus.

As followers of Jesus, we want to become more like him. If we're honest with ourselves, we must admit that, in many ways, we're pretty fuzzy about exactly what it means to be more like him. And anyway, we must surely admit that we are not him! God preserve us from running about self-importantly pronouncing God's blessing, or worse, deluding ourselves into thinking that we are conferring his Spirit, upon unsuspecting souls.

In desiring to breathe out the Spirit upon others, there is no place for an exalted view of ourselves. To the contrary, this is a place where our egos must die. Jesus is the perfume, the incense burning; we are only the smell of it, drifting away in the smoke, and that only because of his sacrifice. But that is enough. If we are open, the Spirit is blowing through us, breathing upon the people we meet.

So that we might be such a blessing to others, we pray:

Lord, open my nostrils,
that I may release what I have inhaled,
and so breathe in your fragrance,
be delighted by it,
and breathe your Spirit upon others.

Remember . . .

- *To Hebrews, Greeks, and Romans, breath and spirit were essentially synonymous.*

- *We are alive, physically and spiritually, because God has breathed his life into us.*

- *We are continually inspiring the stuff of life and death, influences positive and negative, and cues to memories and associations that may affirm or cripple us.*

- *Inhaling the fragrance of God is a deliberate movement toward a deeper intimacy with him. We should not be surprised or disappointed if such an intimacy cannot be quantified or described.*

- *We pray that God will open us up to breathe his Spirit upon others because this fragrance of life can only come from him, the Source of life.*

For Examen (reflection or discussion)

- *What associations of memory or subtle influences around you can you identify as potentially distracting or even dangerous?*

- *Can you identify some way in which God is breathing into you intimacy with him, deliverance, or a more expansive life?*

- *What pleasant odor in your regular life might be conceived as an invitation to a moment of communion with God?*

- *Who has breathed the Spirit into your life? Can you imagine yourself doing so for others?*

5

Open My Mouth

Lord, open my mouth,
that I may release what I have tasted,
and so taste your goodness,
be made strong by the sustenance you give,
and share your sustaining grace with others.

Tasting

My family has been known to fight over food. I remember, as a teenager, bodies flying in the dining room of a friend's house as one dinner party group sought to defend a chocolate torte from the predations of another. It sounds bizarre, and it was—but it was all in good fun. Chocolate torte was my mother's signature fancy dessert: a large meringue shell with rich chocolate mousse filling and a thin layer of hard dark chocolate, all topped with cream whipped thick and stiff. My father used to claim that this would be the final course of that great meal in glory, the Marriage Supper of the Lamb. While that may—it *may*—be hyperbole, chocolate torte has been the crowning taste at every celebratory meal of the Paul clan since I was a kid.

Who doesn't have a favorite food or foods, flavors about which we rhapsodize? I can think of dozens, with no trouble at all. Grilled salmon with Dijon and maple syrup glaze; curried chicken roti; espresso; salted cashews; barbecued sweet potato with a little cinnamon and a lot of butter; Cobblestone Stout; chocolate; sharp old cheddar . . . I could go on. And on, and on.

In a park just a five-minute walk from my house, there is an annual event called RibFest that draws people from all over the city to sample dozens of versions of barbecued ribs. In Malibu, the stretch of beach north of LA that is home or playground to the bright, beautiful, and fabulously wealthy, a chili cook-off is held every Labor Day weekend, attended by a carnival and fair. Think about that for a moment: some of the most famous and privileged people in the world compete to produce a winning version of what likely began as a poor Latina's attempt to make a very little meat go a long way for her hungry family.

One Texas-based website lists almost one hundred BBQ competitions, many with guaranteed financial prizes of as much as $25,000 for the winners. Apparently, taste is taken very seriously indeed in the Lone Star State! The characteristic flavors of certain cuisines seem intrinsic to the cultures from which they have sprung: think of the cream sauces and pastries of French cooking, the tomato sauces and pasta of Italian food, Indian curries, Caribbean jerk, Japanese sushi, the varying spices of Thai, Szechuan, or Mexican food.

For those of us who are privileged to have a range of choices about what we eat, it's worth remembering that, according to the UN, roughly one in eight people in the world are starving;[1] a great many more get by on a subsistence diet of very simple foods like rice or beans—for us, what ends up in our mouths and stomachs is in large measure a function of the particular flavors that we enjoy. Hopefully we have some concern about nutritional value too.

The people who study such things tend to divide tastes into at least four different, basic groups: sweet, sour, salty, and bitter. Recently, there has been a broad acceptance of a newer term, borrowed from the Japanese: *umami*, which means, "delicious taste," refers to the quality of meatiness that renders a steak so attractive to carnivores like me, but as well to foods like tomatoes, mushrooms, fish, and cheeses. Indian and Asian food cultures, not surprisingly, have traditionally added the further category of pungency—what we would usually describe as spicy hotness. Our mouths process these distinct categories of taste in different ways.

They do so by means of between two thousand and five thousand taste buds located primarily in the little bumps that cover our tongues, plus some in the shell of our mouths and at the backs of our throats; each bud has between fifty and one hundred taste receptors.[2] That's why wine or whiskey connoisseurs describe the change in flavors as the liquid moves from the front of the mouth to the back of the throat—the different receptors pick up differing characteristics of what we are tasting.

The bad news is that we lose about half of our taste receptors by twenty years of age. The good news is that this is why a toddler is happy with the blandness of mac and cheese, while an adult can manage and enjoy a spicy burrito.

When we open our mouths to eat, we open ourselves to the food that will sustain us. We need it, can't live without it. And we open our mouths eagerly because we anticipate the sensual delight of the flavor and texture of the food and drink we are about to taste. Most who read this will open themselves up to such sustenance, refreshment, and pleasure several times every day. Each time we do can be a reminder of the One who chose bread and wine as the symbols by which we should remember him.

"Taste and see that the LORD is good," said the psalmist. "The lions may grow weak and hungry, but those who seek the LORD lack no good thing" (Ps. 34:8, 10).

Of course, we use our mouths for a great many other things than tasting: smiling, kissing, breathing, blowing, spitting; holding pens, pins, pipes. Any of these could, I suppose, become the focus of a contemplative exercise, but in these chapters, particularly in *Doing*, we will briefly consider one other use: speaking.

Speech is a powerful instrument for good or ill. With it, the Serpent subverted Adam and Eve. The speeches of Hitler inflamed a civilized nation to war against its neighbors and to systematically exterminate Jews, Roma, communists, gay and lesbian people, and not a few Christians, plus anyone who would protect them.

On the other hand, William Wilberforce's speeches to Parliament propelled Britain to the peaceful abolition of slavery in 1833, some thirty-plus years before the beginning of a particularly bloody civil war to decide the same issue in the United States.

"Our lives begin to end the day we become silent about things that matter," Martin Luther King Jr. said.[3] Who has not heard and been deeply stirred by his famous "I Have a Dream" speech? It's not nearly the same reading the text of it. The patient, measured tones of the early part of the speech, delivered with that precise elocution and yet in a mellifluous Georgia accent; the rising passion that sends a quiver through his voice as he begins to describe his vision of an America where all men, women, and children are truly regarded as equals. The speech is a mere sixteen minutes long, but it motivated a generation to change the nation and still inspires everyone who hears it.

On a more prosaic level, every one of us has had the experience of hurting others or being hurt, encouraging others or being encouraged, simply by virtue of a few words spoken.

Speech, by its very nature, is a reaching out to others, an attempt to bridge the chasm of silence between us. We do not enter upon a contemplative path merely so we can become better individuals, but also so we may become better members of the human family.

The psalm recorded as the last words of King David begins this way: "The Spirit of the LORD spoke through me; his word was on my tongue" (2 Sam. 23:2).

While none of us are likely to become like Hitler or MLK, becoming increasingly open to the movement of God's Spirit within us means having him shape the mode and content of our speech— such that his word may also be on our tongues, as it was on David's.

When we open our mouths to taste, we want to know that what we taste will be good, both pleasing and sustaining. When we open our mouths to speak, we want to know that what we have to say will be good, whether it is challenge or affirmation, reproof or comfort. And so we pray:

Lord, open my mouth,
that I may release what I have tasted,
and so taste your goodness,
be made strong by the sustenance you give,
and share your sustaining grace with others.

Releasing
Lord, open my mouth,
that I may release what I have tasted,
and so taste your goodness,
be made strong by the sustenance you give,
and share your sustaining grace with others.

In 2011, in a thoroughly depressed economy, the top fifteen fast-food chains in the United States sold more than $115 billion worth of food that had been engineered by teams of food scientists to be as cheap and tasty as possible.[4] For these companies, and many others, nutritional value is a consideration only insofar as it motivates customers to purchase their product.

Evidently, one would have to conclude that most of their customers valued concepts like "juicy" over "healthy."

We in the First World are long past eating merely to satisfy a reasonable hunger—that is, to properly nourish our bodies. Obesity has become a health problem of epidemic proportions.

Our taste buds have been trained to prefer foods that are high in unhealthy fats, various forms of sugar, and salt. We are encouraged to "supersize" what we eat, not because our bodies need more calories, but because the habit of stuffing ourselves also stuffs the coffers of large corporations. Our desire for speed and convenience cultivates in us a desire for foods that have been processed into slow, tasty poisons. We are digging our graves with our mouths.

As one who has often spoken of pizza, beer, coffee, and chocolate as the four main food groups, it would be rank hypocrisy for me to lecture anyone on eating well. But at least I can recognize that there is an instructive parallel between the way I feed my body and the way I feed my soul.

As we pray, *Lord, open my mouth, that I may release what I have tasted*, we are asking him to wean us off the unhealthy spiritual foods that bloat our souls and obstruct our spiritual arteries. We are asking him to retrain our taste buds so that our thoughtless craving for spiritual cheese puffs diminishes, and a hunger for real, sustaining, spiritual food grows. (We may be asking that he do the same regarding our taste for material food too!)

As a disappointed apostle Paul wrote to the Corinthians, who had been nibbling on all kinds of spiritual junk food, "Brothers and sisters, I could not address you as people who live by the Spirit but as people who are still worldly—mere infants in Christ. I gave you milk, not solid food, for you were not yet ready for it. Indeed, you are still not ready" (1 Cor. 3:1–2).

Milk, of course, is not a bad food—Paul was just saying that they had not matured as they should have. Sometimes a change in diet is not just a releasing of our preference for nutritionless spiritual snacks but also a function of maturity.

The writer of the letter to the Hebrews also longed to offer the solid food of sustaining words. He challenged the childish dependence of his audience on the familiar and comforting "milk" of the old Jewish religion. Their unwillingness to venture toward the new, spicy flavor of grace was stunting their growth:

> We have much to say about this, but it is hard to make it clear to you because you no longer try to understand. In fact, though by this time you ought to be teachers, you need someone to teach you the elementary truths of God's word all over again. You need milk, not solid food! Anyone who lives on milk, being still an infant, is not acquainted with the teaching about righteousness. But solid food is for the mature. (Heb. 5:11–14)

Are we still only drinking milk—taking a swig now and then of the simple spiritual precepts we were fed as children? Have we not really examined or ventured beyond since then? If this is so, is it any wonder that those precepts sometimes seem less convincing than they once did? What might the solid food on an adult menu taste like?

And what kinds of junk food, I wonder, have we become accustomed to snacking on to take the edge off our true spiritual hunger?

As we try to identify them, we can expect that they also will be processed and prepackaged—fast, easy to get, sweet on the lips. Familiar religious rules, handy judgments, sugary phrases of worship that have no sustaining effect on the way we live our day-to-day lives might be among the snacks that blunt our deeper appetite.

Unless we become open to a new, healthy diet in these areas, our souls will grow flaccid and stunted. But there is a still greater danger. David prayed:

> *Set a guard, O LORD, over my mouth;*
> *keep watch over the door of my lips!*
> *Do not let my heart incline to any evil,*
> *to busy myself with wicked deeds*
> *in company with men who work iniquity,*
> *and let me not eat of their delicacies!* (Ps. 141:3–4 ESV)

David was conscious of the temptation to feed on delicacies—particularly tasty little morsels—that he knew were evil. Solomon expressed similar thoughts in counsel offered to his son, urging him to stay clear of the path of the evil, who "eat the bread of wickedness and drink the wine of violence" (Prov. 4:17 ESV).

Both men, although wise and deeply committed to seeking God, certainly knew whereof they spoke. Both had, at times, dined on wickedness and violence. They knew they remained susceptible to such hungers, and they knew that this food was not just unhealthy but poisonous.

Our society has developed an odd attitude toward these concepts of wickedness, evil, and violence. We can't quite decide whether they're bad, funny, scary, or attractive.

Oh, it's not so difficult when someone shoots up a school full of little children, or abducts and rapes a few young girls for years on end—that's the bad kind of evil for sure. But a movie, TV show, or book about people shooting or robbing or mangling each other? Good fun. Foreigners killing our people? Evil. Our people killing those foreigners? Let freedom reign.

We've certainly been eating some strange fruit. It turns out there's a precedent. "And the LORD God commanded the man, saying, 'You may surely eat of every tree of the garden, but of the tree of the knowledge of good and evil you shall not eat, for in the day that you eat of it you shall surely die'" (Gen. 2:16–17 ESV).

Despite an intimate relationship with a loving, generous Creator, Adam and Eve swallowed the nonsense fed to them by the Serpent—that they could become their own gods. With an entire garden of perfect, wholesome fruit and vegetables to choose from, they picked the one poison fruit instead. After they had eaten, all their new knowledge afforded them was shame, the awareness that they were naked. Out of this shame, this deep awareness of insufficiency and vulnerability, mankind has ever since scrabbled to survive, inflicting violence in the process upon the earth and anyone who is weaker.

We are still being tempted, in a thousand subtle ways, to swallow this sweet morsel with the bitter aftertaste. The pernicious lie that we can be our own gods—that we should always get what we want; that our needs come before those of others; that the rules ought not apply to us—catalyzes with our deeper knowledge that our naked selves are flawed, insufficient, weak. The inevitable result of this spiritual whiplash is violence done to the made-in-God's-imageness of others, as well as our own souls.

We are treading this contemplative path because we are spiritually hungry. We want nourishment that will strengthen us: not junk food that will produce flab rather than muscle, or toxins that will slowly poison us. Mature food, not pablum. We may need to change our diet.

Often the attitudes, entertainments, or even cultural norms that we consume do not strike us as spiritual foods at all—we ingest them in the same semiconscious manner that we might polish off a bag of potato chips while watching TV. We need help, then, to identify and decline those nutritionless or even toxic foods on which our spirits habitually munch. We need help to retune our taste buds so that we develop a genuine hunger for healthy soul food.

And because we need the help of the One who truly *is* God, our God, we pray,

Lord, open my mouth,
that I may release what I have tasted,
and so taste your goodness,
be made strong by the sustenance you give,
and share your sustaining grace with others.

Receiving

Lord, open my mouth,
that I may release what I have tasted,
and so taste your goodness,
be made strong by the sustenance you give,
and share your sustaining grace with others.

For many years now, Annie has been baking the communion bread we share each Sunday at Sanctuary. Sometimes it's a large, round sourdough loaf: crusty and dusty with flour on the outside; soft, white, and tangy on the inside. More often, it's a challah loaf with a braided brown top, glazed with egg wash and sprinkled with sesame seeds. Inside, it's a rich, eggy yellow. Is your mouth watering yet?

It's no surprise, then, that our community members are in the habit of tearing handfuls from the communion bread and munching happily on them as they walk back to their seats. I could make a meal of that bread, washed down with the occasional sip of wine.

This is a bit of a revelation for some visitors, who, like me, grew up pinching a crumb from a loaf that looked and tasted much like one of those sawdust fire logs, or choking down a wafer that seemed designed to suck every drop of moisture and all memory of flavor from our mouths.

I still remember the day, probably fifteen years ago, that my good friend Joe gave thanks for one of those glorious communion loaves. It was a small group that day.

"This bread is really, really tasty," he said to us. "And there's lots of it. Jesus is wonderful, too, and there's more than enough of him to go around. So come and eat. Rip off a big hunk of this bread, and enjoy it."

If it happens that there's any bread left when communion is finished, someone who is hungry will pick up what remains and eat it all up.

What a lovely picture of the sheer enjoyment and fulfilling sustenance to be found in tasting God's goodness!

However did we arrive at the expectation of a dry, bland communion with God under which many of us labor? Consider this invitation from God, spoken through the prophet Isaiah:

> *Come, all you who are thirsty,*
> *come to the waters;*
> *and you who have no money,*
> *come, buy and eat! . . .*
> *Why spend money on what is not bread,*
> *and your labor on what does not satisfy?*
> *Listen, listen to me, and eat what is good,*
> *and you will delight in the richest of fare.* (Isa. 55:1–2)

The salvation to which God invites us is characterized as the best, the healthiest, the most delightful sort of feast. No abstemious beans and rice here, but "the richest of fare."

Thomas à Kempis prayed: "Enlarge Thou me in love, that with the inward palate of my heart I may taste how sweet it is to love, and to be dissolved, and [as it were] to bathe myself in Thy Love."[5]

I wonder if he had been reading the Song of Solomon. As we've noticed already, the language of the poet is redolent with sensual cues. Over and over, the two lovers describe their hungry love for and extravagant delight in each other with descriptors that might more usually be found on the menu of an expensive restaurant.

She:
Let my beloved come to his garden,
and eat its choicest fruits.

He:
I came to my garden, my sister, my bride,
I gathered my myrrh with my spice,
I ate my honeycomb with my honey,
I drank my wine with my milk.

Others:
Eat friends, drink,
and be drunk with love!

He says:
May your breasts be like clusters of grapes on the vine,
the fragrance of your breath like apples,
and your mouth like the best wine.

And she interrupts:

May the wine go straight to my beloved,
flowing gently over lips and teeth.
I belong to my beloved,
and his desire is for me.[6]

Ahem. One feels a bit like a Peeping Tom just reading these passages, so frankly ravenous is the language. And yet, from the earliest Talmudic scholars forward, commentators have agreed that the intended subtext of this voluptuous poetry is the delight God finds in his people and expects them to find in him.

When we pray, *Lord, open my mouth that I may taste your goodness*, we begin to find all around us indications of his presence and blessing. Every bite of something flavorful is a reminder of his desire to enjoy us and to have us enjoy him.

Maggie and I own a sailboat, large enough to sleep aboard, and we enjoy sailing it on Lake Ontario. The sailing itself is a great delight to me, in which I am aware of tasting the Lord's goodness, but there is another pleasure awaiting us when we arrive at a dock or drop anchor in a little bay. Before preparing supper, we break out the wine and cheese: some tangy English Stilton; an old, sharp Quebec cheddar; perhaps some brie; or cream cheese with red pepper jelly on top. We sit there in the cockpit, rocking gently on the water, watching the sun slip down the western sky, nibbling and sipping cheap Italian wine—we are neither of us connoisseurs—and quietly reveling in each other's company.

This is a kind of communion, both between the two of us, and between us and God, of the riches of whose grace we are profoundly aware in such moments. We often remind each other of how extravagantly he has blessed us, and how little we deserve it.

Speaking it aloud reinforces and deepens the thought, opening us further to appreciation of his intimate presence.

These particular times are especially wonderful and conducive, but every normal, humdrum day also presents similar opportunities to commune with others and with God over shared food. *Open us up*, we pray, *to sample the flavors of your goodness in the food we eat and the conversation we share.*

Communion by definition requires more than one person; even the most delectable meal is diminished if eaten alone. As Thomas Merton wrote,

> I will have more joy in heaven and in the contemplation of God, if you are also there to share it with me; and the more of us there will be to share it the greater will be the joy of all. For contemplation is not ultimately perfect unless it is shared. We do not finally taste the full exultation of God's glory until we share His infinite gift.[7]

Imagine the relief of the people of Israel when God provided them with manna and thus saved them from starvation; imagine their further delight when they popped some in their mouths and discovered it tasted *good*. Scripture says it tasted like wafers made with honey when simply picked up and eaten, and like cakes baked with oil (a prized commodity) when milled into flour and baked. Next came succulent little quails: imagine the mouths watering and families calling out to one another from their cooking fires as the smell of the roasting birds wafted through the roving city of hundreds of thousands of people, discussing with delight the surprising new tastes. Communion.

Imagine the tales told, years afterward, by the people who were among the five thousand fed with a young boy's lunch—"Were you there too? I've never forgotten the taste of that fish!"—or the guests at the wedding in Cana: "Best wine ever!" The retelling of those tales would have been in themselves a fresh joy to add to the memory of the flavors. Communion.

One of the key images of the ultimate consummation of all things is the Marriage Supper of the Lamb, in the final chapters of the Revelation. Here the communion of a shared feast is entwined with the communion of two lovers, Christ and his bride, the church, about to consummate their long betrothal.

Perhaps this great love feast to fulfill all love feasts is what Jesus had in mind in the Upper Room when he handed a cup of wine to his disciples and said, "Drink of it, all of you, for this is my blood of the covenant, which is poured out for many for the forgiveness of sins. I tell you I will not drink again of this fruit of the vine until that day when I drink it new with you in my Father's kingdom" (Matt. 26:27–29 ESV).

Won't that be a prime vintage? My friend Chuck has, on a couple of occasions, shared with Maggie and me a bottle of his favorite California wine. Chuck knows a lot about wine. My own palate might be generously described as "uneducated," but even I could tell that this was far, far superior to the plonk we normally drink. Sipping it, I was grateful for the wonderful taste in the moment; remembering it, I appreciate Chuck's generosity, and look forward to lifting a cup of the finest vintage ever with the one who calls himself the True Vine.

By such simple experiences, and the even more common ones of daily routine, barely noticed—a morning espresso, a square of chocolate in the middle of the afternoon—we are having our spiritual taste buds attuned to a deeper communion with our Creator and Lover, with ourselves, with one another, and with the world around us.

Peter wrote, "Like newborn babies, crave pure spiritual milk

[Start simply! Give your taste buds a chance!], so that by it you may grow up in your salvation, now that you have tasted that the Lord is good" (1 Peter 2:2–3).

Peter had learned a thing or two about having his tastes changed. The writer of the Acts told us how, while hungry and waiting for dinner, Peter began to pray. He fell into a trance and saw, coming down from above, a sheet stretched out, full of animals the Jews considered unclean. A voice told him to eat, but Peter, a good Jew, refused. "I have never eaten anything impure or unclean," he said.

The voice spoke again: "Do not call anything impure that God has made clean" (10:14–15).

The reason for the vision became clear a short time later, when messengers arrived from the soldier who had command of the Roman forces occupying Judea. This Cornelius was both pagan and oppressor—the epitome of an enemy to a Jewish patriot—and yet Peter was soon spreading out the feast of God's grace before him and his household. For the first time, Peter realized that Jesus wasn't just for good Jews, but for everyone, regardless of ethnicity, morality, religion, or any other qualifier.

It wasn't just a new flavor for the Roman. Peter's palate, his communion, was suddenly, wonderfully expanded too. "I now realize," he said, "how true it is that God does not show favoritism but accepts people from every nation" (10:34–35).

There are people who only ever want to eat the same old meatloaf and mashed potatoes (or their equivalents). But we are on this path because we want to be able to discern the subtle herbs and to savor the riotous spices—sometimes familiar but often new, and always expanding—with which God flavors the rich meal of our communion together and with him.

And so, as the food and drink of which we partake reminds us, we pray:

Lord, open my mouth,
that I may release what I have tasted,
and so taste your goodness,
be made strong by the sustenance you give,
and share your sustaining grace with others.

Becoming

Lord, open my mouth,
that I may release what I have tasted,
and so taste your goodness,
be made strong by the sustenance you give,
and share your sustaining grace with others.

When we are introducing our celebration of the Lord's Supper at Sanctuary each week, we often include a few phrases like these:

We have not come to this table because we have our lives sorted out or cleaned up.

We don't come because we think we deserve it.

We come because we are hungry and thirsty for food that will sustain our souls, and we know that without it we will die.

Speaking to one another about what the bread and wine mean to us, and how they will nourish us, prepares us to appreciate more fully the value of what we are about to consume. We experience something similar in the context of common meals: "Oh, that salmon is good! What is in the glaze?" "Is that cumin I taste?" "Carrot cake! I'm glad I left room . . ."

As pleasurable as good food and drink are, and although that pleasure is in itself a great good, pleasure alone cannot direct our dietary choices without serious, even life-threatening, consequences. We pray that *I may release what I have tasted* because we recognize that we may easily fill up our souls with nutritionless junk; we pray *and so taste your goodness* because we want to learn to delight in the many flavors of God's grace.

But now we pray that we may *be made strong by the sustenance you give* because we know that we must either grow or shrivel: become healthier, more limber, more powerful—or wither away.

David had been anointed the next king of Israel, but he found himself being hunted in the desert by the jealous King Saul. He knew that the anointing wasn't enough; he needed physical and spiritual food to sustain him until the time God would deliver him the throne. During that difficult time, he wrote,

> *O God, you are my God, earnestly I seek you;*
> *my soul thirsts for you;*
> *my flesh faints for you,*
> *as in a dry and weary land where there is no water. . . .*
>
> *My soul will be satisfied as with fat and rich food,*
> *and my mouth will praise you with joyful lips.*
> (Ps. 63:1, 5 ESV)

Hunger is a reminder that we need food. It's usually when we eat *past* our hunger—that is, we routinely eat for the sake of the sensual experience and never pause long enough between meals to actually feel hungry—that we begin to eat junk that is long on flavor and short on nutritional value. Perhaps, in a First World context where food is so plentiful for most of us, we need to cultivate some measure of hunger before sitting down to a healthy meal.

Like many other contemplative writers, Thomas Merton encouraged us to do exactly this with regard to our spiritual appetites: "Do not look for pleasure, but turn away from things that satisfy your senses and your mind and look for God in hunger and thirst and darkness, through deserts of the spirit in which it seems to be madness to travel."[8]

We must not be afraid to admit to ourselves the character and scope of our deep spiritual hungers. Sating ourselves with cheap pleasures will keep us from doing so, and from seeking out the food that will make us strong. But it is not an easy thing to set aside the distractions that dull our senses and begin a journey into the desert areas of our own souls.

We may find there hungers that we have never fulfilled: longings to be fully known and deeply loved, utterly accepted. Fears and insecurities may assail us: *If anyone knew who I really am, I would be rejected, driven out. If I do not appear strong, I will be taken advantage of. I have nothing of value to offer.*

We may come face-to-face with pathetic dependencies we have long avoided acknowledging: *I drink or eat too much. I watch TV or surf the net for hours. I work many hours more than I need to. I accumulate money and goods insatiably. I go to church and pretend that I'm all right—all to avoid the great void in my own heart, my deep disappointment with life or with my spouse, with my friends or family or lack of success or with God.*

When the people of Israel, long acclimated to slavery, were about to set out into such a desert, God prescribed a meal to strengthen them for the journey. Roast lamb, bitter herbs (traditionally horseradish and romaine lettuce, but including a wide range of green leaf and root vegetables), flat bread. Wine, of course, and water. It was a healthy, sustaining meal, to be eaten fully clothed, standing up, with sandals strapped on and staves in hand. Ready to leave the homes they had known, such as they were, and set out into the unknown wild places.

They were leaving slavery too; and that, as we have already seen, turned out to be more difficult than might be imagined. God instructed the people to re-enact and eat this Passover meal each year as a reminder they had been set free, at a cost, and that whatever challenges they faced currently, they were the people of God. It must have been a welcome break, too, from the usual fare of manna and quail!

The Eucharist also reminds us of who we are—the redeemed people of God—and that our sustenance for the journey is the Lamb of God, Jesus himself. We may study theology, advocate for social justice, preach to others, give generously, and even partake of the communion bread and cup without really feeding on Jesus.

In a rather lengthy discussion with a group of excited people who thought they had seen something numinous in his miraculous feeding of thousands, Jesus repeatedly referred to himself as food—"true bread from heaven"; "the bread of God"; "the bread of life." His listeners asked him to give them some of that bread, but instead he kept talking about who he is. Understandably, they began to grumble: "Why doesn't he just give us some? How can he claim to be this sustaining food?"

Jesus didn't answer them directly. Instead, he repeated, "I am the living bread that came down from heaven. Whoever eats this bread will live forever. This bread is my flesh, which I will give for the life of the world" (John 6:51).

His listeners were left to argue among themselves: "How can this man give us his flesh to eat?" (v. 52).

A good question, that. How, exactly? Since Jesus never told them, we must accept that partaking of him is a mystery, not to be approached with a sheet of DIY instructions, but in faith. In openness. The words of the psalm writer Asaph are helpful here:

I am the LORD your God,
who brought you up out of Egypt.
Open wide your mouth and I will fill it. (Ps. 81:10)

Two things appear necessary: remembering just who our Deliverer and Sustainer is, and opening our mouths wide. We stretch our necks toward him like baby birds to their mother, not understanding the provenance of the food that strengthens us, but trusting the source.

Is it possible to lose sight of Jesus, not only along the meandering footpaths of ordinary life but also among the thickets of doctrine, religious tradition, or church practice and politics? When I have been reading theology, or contemplative literature, or even other places in Scripture (let alone the novels to which I am addicted), I return always with a sense of relief to the Gospels, where the bewilderingly complex Jesus is presented nevertheless with such clarity. It's like sitting down to a favorite home-cooked meal after a week or two of eating in restaurants.

The truth is that, without Jesus, I'm personally not much interested in God or religion. God seems unreachable at best, and perhaps uninterested or nonexistent; and religious observance seems irrelevant. Although the more I learn about him, the more I realize I have yet to learn, I can trust Jesus because he, too, has traversed the desert through which I am wandering.

He knows what it's like to be afraid, uncertain. Hungry. Homeless, abandoned, betrayed, beaten, in pain. Frustrated with friends and loved ones who just don't get it. Angry, hurt, and puzzled by the apparent indifference of God at the most critical moments: *Why have you forsaken me?* He knows what it's like to be human.

It is this Jesus—who trudges beside me along the dusty, boring, tiring, at times seemingly pointless wilderness path—who feeds and sustains me. It is he who gives me enough strength to hope in the transcendent, in resurrection, and in a God who is love.

He says to us, "I am the vine; you are the branches. If you remain in me and I in you, you will bear much fruit; apart from me you can do nothing" (John 15:5).

We are drinking up the good, sustaining nutrients that are drawn up through the very roots of the Vine, along its strong stalk, and so delivered into us. Small and tender though we may be, we want every fiber to be wide open to the food he offers, so that we may grow strong and be fruitful.

As we take in this good spiritual food, what comes out of our mouths will be changed too. The kind of words we speak will be part of the fruit we bear—worship to God and blessing to others.

This is why we pray:

> Lord, open my mouth,
> that I may release what I have tasted,
> and so taste your goodness,
> *be made strong by the sustenance you give,*
> and share your sustaining grace with others.

Doing

> Lord, open my mouth,
> that I may release what I have tasted,
> and so taste your goodness,
> be made strong by the sustenance you give,
> *and share your sustaining grace with others.*

On the long hike from Judea in the south back to their Galilean homes in the north, Jesus and his disciples made a short detour to view a tourist attraction. Although not mentioned explicitly in the

Old Testament, everyone in that part of the world agreed that the ancient well outside the town of Sychar had been hewn deep into solid rock by the patriarch Jacob himself.

The town, known once as Shechem, was one of the Cities of Refuge granted to the priestly tribe of the Levites when they entered the promised land of Canaan; and it lay in a territory now called Samaria. One of the few matters upon which Samaritans and Jews were agreed was that Jacob—who wrestled an angel through the night and came away crippled but blessed, and with a new name: Israel—was their forefather.

The Samaritans were descended from the people who had been left behind when King Nebuchadnezzar took the elite of the Hebrews into exile in Babylon. According to the Jews who returned seventy years later, those who had been left in the land had intermarried with surrounding tribes and in the interim developed a perverse version of Hebrew worship.

The Samaritans believed that it was the returning Jews who had brought back illicit religious practices from Babylon and who no longer adhered to the true faith.

To put it into a modern perspective, the part of Samaria in which Sychar was located is now called the West Bank, where Israelis and Palestinians—both Semitic peoples, claiming Abraham as their forefather—do battle over what both consider an ancient homeland, fueled by their religious differences and historical grievances.

Imagine, then, an Israeli Jesus found deep in conversation with a Palestinian woman by his disciples. They had made a foray into town for groceries; in the meantime, the woman had slaked Jesus' thirst by drawing water from the well, and now he was slaking hers by speaking words of life. The disciples were so surprised by the scenario that they couldn't bring themselves to question either their Master or the interloper about what was going on. Eager to share what she had heard, the woman soon headed home.

"Meanwhile his disciples urged him, 'Rabbi, eat something.' But he said to them, 'I have food to eat that you know nothing about.' Then his disciples said to each other, 'Could someone have brought him food?' 'My food,' said Jesus, 'is to do the will of him who sent me and to finish his work'" (John 4:31–34).

We pray that God will open our mouths to *share his sustaining grace with others* because doing his will is not just fulfilling a duty. It is an expression of communion with him and with other people—a communion quenching our thirst and hunger, as well as that of the people with whom we seek to share.

It's no mistake that Jesus said this about his conversation with a woman whom most Jews would have despised and dismissed. It's no coincidence that he was willing to drink the water she gave him as well as offering her "water welling up to eternal life" (v. 14). His conversation with her was food to him, just as it was to her.

It's not that hard to figure out the will of the One who sent Jesus. We don't need to spend a lot of time praying, "Lord, what shall I do?" The entire biblical story is about seeking out the broken ones—if we are honest with ourselves, we will find ourselves right there with the Samaritan woman—and welcoming them in.

While at the home of a wealthy and powerful religious leader for a meal, Jesus remarked, "When you give a luncheon or dinner, do not invite your friends, your brothers or sisters, your relatives, or your rich neighbors; if you do, they may invite you back and so you will be repaid. But when you give a banquet, invite the poor, the crippled, the lame, the blind, and you will be blessed" (Luke 14:12–14).

In opening up to give, we also are filled. It's worth noting that this isn't just about writing a check—although checks must certainly be written to fund any banquet! Nor is it about providing the minimum, a bag lunch. It's about real, rich, deep human connection with people who are in need. We will even find there is room for our own hungry souls at the table! In such connection, we may share food as well as the sustenance of words that are encouraging, affirming, blessing—and both will provide nourishment.

Jesus went on to tell a story about a man who threw a party— and no one came. All his wealthy friends declined, so he directed his servant to go into the streets and alleys and bring back the city's rejects. This, then, is the work the servants of the One who sent Jesus should be doing. Offering words of invitation to those who are excluded; food to the hungry; refreshing drink to the thirsty.

Speaking through the prophet Isaiah, God makes it clear that sharing what we ourselves have received is not only how we enact kingdom justice but also the deepest form of worship.

> *Is this the kind of fast [religious*
> *   observance] I have chosen,*
> *only a day for people to humble themselves?*
> *Is it only for bowing one's head like a reed? . . .*
>
> *Is not this the kind of fasting I have chosen:*
> *to loose the chains of injustice*
> *and untie the cords of the yoke,*
> *to set the oppressed free*
> *and break every yoke?*
> *Is it not to share your food with the hungry*
> *and to provide the poor wanderer with shelter—*
> *when you see the naked, to clothe them,*
> *and not to turn away from your own flesh and blood?*
>   (Isa. 58:5–7)

Perhaps in our churches we worry too much about relevant worship styles. Perhaps we spend simply too much time, energy, and money on and in our church buildings! Perhaps instead we should be worshipping by sharing our food with people who are hungry. Perhaps we should be using our mouths to speak up for those who are oppressed and finding ways of helping them speak for themselves. Perhaps we should be speaking words of blessing and affirmation to people whose lives are messed up—we won't have to look far to find them! We could open our mouths to welcome in the ones who are always left out, calling them brothers and sisters. This would be a generous openness!

People who have not experienced the peculiar joy of sharing their food with the hungry may worry that the experience will exhaust rather than fill them up. God, in this same Isaiah passage, promises otherwise:

> *If you spend yourselves in behalf of the hungry*
> *and satisfy the needs of the oppressed,*
> *then your light will rise in the darkness,*
> *and your night will become like the noonday.*
> *The* LORD *will guide you always;*
> *he will satisfy your needs in a sun-scorched land*
> *and will strengthen your frame.* (Isa. 58:10–11)

In the economy of God's kingdom, the one who gives always gains.

Jesus, visiting the synagogue in his hometown of Nazareth, read his own mission statement from Isaiah 61, a mission statement that ought also to be ours:

The Spirit of the Lord is on me,
because he has anointed me
to proclaim good news to the poor.
He has sent me to proclaim freedom for the prisoners
and recovery of sight for the blind,
to set the oppressed free,
to proclaim the year of the Lord's favor. (Luke 4:18–19)

And young Hebrew king Lemuel recorded the admonition of his wise mother:

Open your mouth for the mute,
for the rights of all who are destitute.
Open your mouth, judge righteously,
defend the rights of the poor and needy. (Prov. 31:8–9 ESV)

We might well worry that we won't know what to say—that, like Moses, we "have never been eloquent"—but we need not, for Jesus himself promises us that even under the most dire circumstances, "I will give you a mouth and wisdom, which none of your adversaries will be able to withstand or contradict" (Luke 21:15 ESV).

We need only ask him to open our mouths and trust that he will fill them.

There is one other, very sweet gift that comes to us when we dare to be open enough to share with others the sustaining grace we have experienced. Do you remember, back in the chapter about opening our eyes, the story Jesus told of the end of time, when those who have cared for the outcast will realize that they have cared for him? "For I was hungry and you gave me something to eat, I was thirsty and you gave me something to drink" (Matt. 25:35).

The invitation to share our own food and drink with hungry, thirsty people is an invitation to dine with the King. Announcing the good news of God's grace to the poor is a means of sharing the mission of the Messiah. This is a mystery, and for many, an intimidating one. We need help to step beyond the protections of our privilege, beyond the vulnerability of our insecurities. And so we pray:

> Lord, open my mouth,
> that I may release what I have tasted,
> and so taste your goodness,
> be made strong by the sustenance you give,
> *and share your sustaining grace with others.*

Remember . . .

- *One in every eight people in the world is starving.*
- *A healthy spiritual diet requires as much intentionality as does a healthy food diet.*
- *God's intention is that "your soul will delight in the richest of fare."*
- *God delights in his communion with us and expects that we will also delight in communion with him.*

For Examen (reflection or discussion)

- *Can you identify unhealthy spiritual "foods" to which you habitually turn?*
- *How have you tasted God's grace in the past few days?*

- *What simple, daily communion—sharing food and drink with someone you care about—might be a previously unnoticed opportunity to create space for God at the table?*

- *How, in spiritual and material terms, might you share your own food and drink with people who are hungry and thirsty? If you are doing so already, can you identify ways in which Jesus is or has been present to you in that circumstance?*

6

Open My Hands

Lord, open my hands,
that I may release what I have held,
and so hold what you give me,
be molded by your touch,
and reach out to others.

TOUCHING

If the demon-possessed maniac who once roamed the tombs of Gadara had been raised from the dead and sent to haunt us, he would surely have looked and sounded much like this.

A stocky man with wild, tangled hair and filthy clothes that seemed eager to be shed of the one who wore them: his shirt gaped, his beltless pants kept slipping down his naked thighs, his shoes were split and bound with fraying duct tape. His face was smeared with black, white, and red greasepaint. He had swept into our worship gathering like a foul and capricious wind, and he stood, swaying dangerously, beside the communion table.

He put his head back and howled at the ceiling—animal noises—then screamed that he was Satan, he was Hitler, he was the Joker. He delighted in destruction, he would kill us all, burn down the building. Then he threw himself to the floor and lay there twitching and moaning.

To be honest, none of this would be all that unusual at a Sanctuary drop-in, but it did make it challenging to focus on worship.

It took a while to get him off the floor onto his feet and then move him out of the building—shrieking threats and foaming at the mouth all the while. He was still new to the community then, and I had no idea what he would do once I got him outside. Half expecting he would attack me, I stood ready.

The noise and fury dissipated in seconds. He turned toward me, and instead of throwing the punch I was waiting for, he put his head on my chest and burst into tears. There was nothing to do but hold him. My arms around him, my hands on his heaving back.

I, too, have been held.

My earliest memory is of my father holding me, a toddler, in his arms in the shower. I remember him embracing me when, as a twelve-year-old, my dog died, and again many years later, the last time he reached out to touch me before he died. I can still feel Henri Nouwen's thumb tracing the sign of the cross on my forehead and the lightness of his hands on my shoulder blades. I recall the touch of the chubby little digits of my own children when they were still infants, grasping my ear, my nose, my lip; and Maggie's slender fingers, splayed across my lower back, drawing me close for a last hug and kiss before I left home this very morning.

I was the youngest child by four years and quite close to my mother. Strangely, although she surely must have held me closer and more often and tenderly than anyone else through the first ten or fifteen years of my life, I have no specific memory of her embracing me as a child. I can only think this is because her touch was so frequent, so necessary, and so entirely taken for granted, that I became as oblivious to it as I am to the air I breathe.

The wild man who interrupted our worship that day has since become a dear friend, bumping his fist against mine or hugging me several times each week. I wonder, was he held by his mother as I was by mine?

We may experience the sensations of touching or being touched with any part of our skin. It's our largest organ, typically between sixteen and twenty-one square feet on an adult. Each square inch contains, on average, more than a thousand nerve endings; we are often able to feel the infinitesimal pressure caused by a barely visible bug alighting on a hair on our arm. We touch with our entire bodies; we hold with our arms and, especially, our hands.

We are not likely to be touched or held ourselves, nor to touch or hold others in any fulfilling way, if we approach life with fists clenched. Rabbi Meir wrote, "We come into the world with clenched fists, as though to say, 'The whole world is mine to acquire.' We leave the world with hands wide open, as though to say, 'I have acquired nothing in this world.'"[1]

Is it true that we acquire nothing in this world? Certainly we can take nothing material out of it, but this only tells us that it's not the material of this world that truly matters. Another version of this saying might be, "We are born with our hands clenched, and spend the rest of our lives learning to open them up."

There is a world of difference between touching with the knuckles of a swinging fist and touching with an outstretched fingertip. There is a subtle difference between clutching and holding. We want open hands, with which to touch, to hold and release, to receive the many gifts life has to offer, and to pass them on to others. Almost any gift is made greater when it is shared. I think there is a great deal worth acquiring in this world; but we cannot do so with our fingers folded tightly into our palms, or while clutching tightly what we already have.

And we want to open our hands and arms so that we may be touched and held ourselves. Infants do not thrive if they are not gently held—if they are not tenderly stroked and tickled and nibbled and kissed. The absence of such nurture can result in a lifetime of emotional and psychological challenge. Even as adults, we still need to be touched and held, confident that we are safe and beloved, in order to truly become the people God has made us to be.

The difficulties of life may so batter us that instead of opening up, we instinctively clutch to ourselves those few familiar treasures—sometimes we think they are treasures simply because they *are* familiar—that are most precious to us, afraid that if we lose them, we will lose ourselves. It takes courage and mature faith to trust that, as Jesus teaches us, "whoever loses his life for my sake will find it" (Matt. 10:39 ESV).

We say our lives are in God's hands, and this, thankfully, is ultimately true. And yet, as Jesus intimates, God also allows us in some measure to hang on to our lives ourselves. He is patiently waiting for us to relax our white-knuckled grip so that we can receive a new kind of life: eternal life. This is not just a life that carries on past physical death, but a life that is, here and now, increasingly open to the infinite scope of the Creator and Sustainer of the universe.

We have set out on this contemplative path in part because something within us longs to release the worries and concerns that we sense are, from an eternal perspective, quite small. Some instinct tells us that this is the way to live a more expansive life. But the world we live in has trained us to grasp at what we can, to come out swinging. It's difficult to change those impulses. In fact, we have found that we cannot do so on our own.

That is why we pray:

> *Lord, open my hands,*
> that I may release what I have held,
> and so hold what you give me,
> be molded by your touch,
> and reach out to others.

Releasing

Lord, open my hands,
that I may release what I have held,
and so hold what you give me,
be molded by your touch,
and reach out to others.

When I was a child, I remember hearing a story about how some Asian hunters catch monkeys. A gourd is hollowed out, and a hole cut in the top just big enough for a monkey to slip his little hand into it. The gourd is secured by a short length of vine to the base of a nearby tree—perhaps the very one in which the monkey and his troop sleep. The hunter places a ball of sweetened rice, or some other food monkeys like, into the gourd and retreats a little distance to wait.

The monkey, having watched all the preparations, is curious. Once he is confident that the hunter is far enough away, he descends from the tree, picks up the gourd, and smells the tasty treat within. He reaches into the gourd and grabs it, but with the food in his fist, he is unable to withdraw his hand. Because he (why is it I always imagine this monkey is male?) is unwilling to let go of his prize, and the vine won't let him scamper off with the gourd still around his fist, it's an easy matter for the hunter to step up and nab him. The story may be apocryphal,[2] but it's a good analogy of how we may be trapped, enslaved, and even consumed—some hunters apparently love a good monkey stew—by clinging to the things that we value.

There are many specific things we might do well to let go of. And we should remember that letting go may not always be about dropping something or throwing it away. It may more often mean holding it lightly enough in our hands that God can move it, or remove it, as he sees fit. Even this is not easy.

We'll consider four general aspects of our lives where we need to open our hands and release our grip: our certainties, agendas, accomplishments, and possessions.

Matthew's gospel recounts how, when Jesus began to try to explain to his disciples that he would soon be taken, tried, killed, and raised back to life, Peter objected. "Never, Lord!" he said. "This shall never happen to you!" (Matt. 16:22).

Peter had just before this made his great confession of Jesus as the Messiah, the Son of the Living God. Jesus had affirmed Peter's conviction as being a revelation from God and asserted that upon the foundation of these truths, he would build his church. No wonder Peter was certain that his Master could never be taken and killed!

Certainty is seductive. All of us have a deep desire to know at least a few things *for sure*. Some people seem to know everything for sure! And others mistake certainty for faith. We may hold fast to our convictions in matters of religious doctrine, or politics, or who is at fault in a personal conflict, and believe that by clinging tenaciously to those beliefs we are being true to ourselves, our country, our God.

But such certainty is the enemy of faith, and the enemy of openness. Faith can only really grow in the presence of uncertainty: when we are absolutely sure, we are, finally, trusting our own judgment rather than God's faithfulness. We are no longer open to the possibility that he will move in a different direction—one that we, with our radically finite capacities, are unable to deduce from past experience.

Who would have believed, before it actually happened, that God could die?

At the foot of the cross, every certainty of the disciples who had dedicated their lives to following Jesus was smashed. They had no choice but to let go of everything they had clung to. As the body of their Master was placed in the tomb, they were unable to imagine how God would soon redeem an apparently impossible situation.

When we cling to our certainties, we are closed to the gifts others may hand us—new perspectives, approaches, abilities, modes of doing or being. Peter's later certainty that he, at least, would never abandon Jesus would also be pried from his bulldog grip. That "failure" became the defining moment for the rest of his life—a life in which he learned to trust God rather than his own convictions. His failure, it turned out, was a gift.

Jesus' reaction to Peter's "Never, Lord!" was unequivocal and couched in the harshest language he ever used: "Get behind me, Satan! You are a stumbling block to me; you do not have in mind the concerns of God, but merely human concerns" (v. 23).

Perhaps even Jesus found Peter's certainty to be dangerously tempting.[3] The last thing he needed was a close friend telling him he didn't really need to go to the cross! Is it possible that his friend's seductive words returned to haunt him as he sweat drops of blood in Gethsemane?

A moment after delivering this stinging rebuke, he turned to the disciples to explain that following him would look much different from what they had been imagining: "Whoever wants to be my disciple must deny themselves and take up their cross and follow me. For whoever wants to save their life will lose it, but whoever loses their life for me will find it. What good will it be for someone to gain the whole world, yet forfeit their soul?" (vv. 24–26).

By insisting that we must deny ourselves, Jesus is calling us to release our grip on our own agendas. Just as Peter and the others had plans and expectations about how the kingdom would come about (Jesus triumphantly acclaimed as king), what it would look like (freedom from the Romans, a return to power and prominence for Israel), and what their own roles within it would be (sitting at the right and left hand of the King!), we, too, are busily plotting our own courses. This is especially true when we believe we're engaged in doing good and things are moving smoothly along in our lives. "Success" seems to confirm that we are in the right, just as Jesus' momentary popularity seemed to confirm to the disciples that their own goals were in line with those of their Master.

Given their understanding and context, the disciples' agenda was reasonable, and even laudable. But it wasn't God's agenda. Despite all Jesus' teaching about the character of the kingdom he had come to announce, they had failed to grasp the essence of it. After his resurrection, Jesus gently warned Peter that he would never even have control over his own personal agenda, let alone that of God's kingdom: "When you are old you will stretch out your hands, and someone else will dress you and lead you where you do not want to go" (John 21:18).

Jesus was calling Peter to trust God's agenda for his life, even if it led ultimately to martyrdom. He is calling us to stretch out our hands, too, with our plans and expectations lying loose on open palms.

Taking up our crosses and losing our lives means dying to the internal record of the accomplishments we think define us as people of value or importance. Jesus' death—rather than his teaching, miracles, or even his resurrection—is the fulcrum of his own life and work, as well as the establishment of the kingdom of God. Both his ministry and resurrection were and are essential, of course; but without his sacrificial death, the former would have long since faded into insignificance, and the latter would have been impossible.

We come to God with open hands because we have nothing to give him—nothing we know, or plan, or have done, or have gained. We have only ourselves to offer, and this is all he wants. We can lose our lives to God, release everything we think we are and have, and we gain everything. Only then do our accomplishments have any real meaning at all.

Finally, Jesus challenges our valuing of the possessions that often drive our accomplishments and agendas and give material shape to our certainties.

What good will it be for someone to gain the whole world, yet forfeit their soul?

Never in the history of the world have people had the sheer volume of stuff that we in the First World have accrued and are busy still accruing. As the bumper sticker says, tongue-only-partly-in-cheek, "The one who dies with the most toys wins." Has there ever been a clearer demonstration of the owner being owned by what he owns than the way mobile phones have permeated every area and aspect of our lives?

We are driven by our addiction to *more* and have lost our capacity to be joyfully content with *enough*. As long as we compulsively seek more, we will never have enough. As long as those of us who already have more than we need continue to demand still more, those who do not have enough will never have what they need. If we ever learn to be content with enough, there will be more than enough for all.

We need to loosen our grip on the things we own so that their grip on us might also be released. We need to learn how to be content with what we have, to approach the acquisition of new things with open rather than grasping hands.

Clearly, opening our hands in these ways is countercultural.

Doing so may be interpreted by others as a lack of ambition or pride, as weak or unrealistic or stupid. It may even feel like that to us. As we pray, *Lord, open our hands,* we will likely find the challenge of releasing our grip on our certainties, agendas, accomplishments, and possessions all but insurmountable.

How encouraging to know, then, that the One who himself gave up everything, who "though he was in the form of God, did not count [even!] equality with God a thing to be grasped [clutched to himself],"[4] is just waiting for us to ask:

> Lord, open my hands,
> *that I may release what I have held,*
> and so hold what you give me,
> be molded by your touch,
> and reach out to others.

Receiving

> Lord, open my hands,
> that I may release what I have held,
> *and so hold what you give me,*
> be molded by your touch,
> and reach out to others.

Really, in opening our hands to let go of what we have clutched, we are giving ourselves into the hands of God. We are releasing our grip on the scrap of wreckage to which we have clung in the belief that it will keep us from drowning in an angry sea and allowing our Rescuer to haul us into the boat. This sounds like it should be easy, even a relief, but that moment of letting go is usually terrifying: What if he loses his grip as we are loosening ours? What if his attention is elsewhere at that moment, and he's not reaching out for us at all?

And what exactly will he give us if we let go of the things we have prized—or in which, at least, we have felt secure? Will they be as good as the things we have now? As comfortable and comforting?

The truth, of course, is that if he is the good God we trust he is, these questions are ultimately absurd. Ultimately—but not necessarily immediately, as we shall see. It still takes faith, and perhaps some measure of courage, to let go of that scrap of wreckage.

As we pray, *Lord, open my hands to receive and hold what you give me*, we might find ourselves wondering, *What will I touch today that will remind me of the gifts God gives? And what are the gifts themselves?*

Practically anything could be such a reminder, couldn't it? The softness of my wife's cheek under my fingertips a few seconds after the alarm has gone off. The heat radiating into my palm from the glorious cup of espresso (black gold!) as I raise it to my lips. The pebbled leather of a jacket I love, the dog's fur, the rubber grips on my bicycle's handle bars, the weight of a valued tool in my hand, the solid warmth of a friend's handshake or hug.

But if these things—all pleasant to the touch—are gifts, what about experiences that are painful? While writing the preceding chapters, I had a mishap on my bike, breaking my collarbone and separating my shoulder. It hurt quite a bit at the time, and it is still stiff and sore several weeks later. Is this a gift too?

These *are* all gifts in themselves, both the pleasurable and the painful, and they point to still greater gifts.

James tells us, "Every good and perfect gift is from above, coming down from the Father of the heavenly lights, who does not change like shifting shadows" (1:17).

When Maggie and I were married, we received as a wedding gift a very large and old Bible. I imagine that it was originally a pulpit Bible, or perhaps a family Bible from another age, although there were no names or dates written in it. I remember joking with the givers about the weight of it, pretending I could barely hold it.

But I did hold it. I opened it carefully, after caressing the cover and remarking on the elaborate leather binding, almost black with age. I stroked the pages, turning through them slowly while my proud benefactors watched. We talked about the book's provenance and where I would keep it when I got it home; whether Maggie would be as pleased and impressed as I was. (Of course!)

The Bible is too big and too delicate for me to ever really use. It employs a translation that, while poetic, is unwieldy for modern exegesis. But I will hold on to that Bible until the day I die.

The two men who gave it to me have, for most of the many years I've known them, been homeless. Both are addicts. Neither would likely describe himself as Christian. I've had more than my share of conflict with both of them, and I'm sure there will be more in the future. I have often been angry with them, and they have hurled threats and epithets at me that I would never repeat.

In spite of all that, they gave me the Bible because they love me, and they know that I love them. The value of the gift is not, mostly, in itself, but in the givers. Their gift reminds me of the deeper truth of our relationship.

When we forget to value the one who gives us a gift, we tend to consume rather than hold what we have been given. That is, we enjoy it for a moment—then quickly move on to seeking the next sensual pleasure, like a child at Christmas tearing through one package after another. The deeper value of a more intimate connection with the giver is lost.

Each time we hold the things that are precious or pleasurable, may the experience remind us that, whether it's someone we love, or a leather jacket, or an old Bible, it is communicating to us the unsearchable riches of the grace of the Giver.

Perhaps the reason we so easily forget this is that many of us are afflicted with a residual feeling that pleasure is bad, or at least separate from God—who, we suspect, is a very, very serious dude with a laser focus on *getting things done* as efficiently as possible, who has hands like oak planks, and who never, ever sleeps in. A Regimental Sergeant Major sort of character.

The psalmist knew better: "You make known to me the path of life; in your presence there is fullness of joy; at your right hand are pleasures forevermore" (Ps. 16:11 ESV).

As we pray, *Lord, open our hands,* and become more intentionally aware of the simple pleasures of touch we receive day by day, each one can become a means of putting our own hands into the hand of the Giver.

What about pain, then? Could we dare to receive the painful experiences of life as gifts of God, or should we just credit him for the pleasant stuff and ascribe all else to malign influence (It was the devil!), our own fault (I can be such a bozo!), or mere happenstance (Stuff happens!)?

It's good to remember James's assertion that God's gifts are both good and perfect (complete) and that his character is unchanging. We must determine to trust its truthfulness, because the goodness and perfection of some of the gifts we receive are not immediately apparent. In fact, they may seem anything but good and perfect—pain, for instance. We have to trust that they will ultimately be so, because God is never less than good.

We understandably and quite sensibly avoid pain. Medieval Christians often seemed to seek it, taking literally Paul's injunction to "mortify therefore your members which are upon the earth" (Col. 3:5 KJV). The Rule of Benedict is still followed in a general way not only by Benedictine monks, like the good monks of Quarr Abbey, but also a variety of intentional Christian communities. In several places it blandly advocates the "harsh beatings" of young novices "to cure them." (Beating older monks is prohibited, unless the abbot has given permission. *Whew!*) Various flagellant movements, eventually condemned by the Roman Catholic Church as heretical, arose from the thirteenth century and onward; adherents beat themselves bloody in order to attain God's favor. Strange God.

Life is quite full enough of pain without self-flagellation or the disciplinary beating of others. While it would be foolish to seek pain, we must learn to hold the experience of it as another kind of gift from God. Consider the following words from Paul, who knew a thing or two about pain himself: "The Spirit himself bears witness with our spirit that we are children of God, and if children, then heirs—heirs of God and fellow heirs with Christ, provided we suffer with him in order that we may also be glorified with him. For I consider that the sufferings of this present time are not worth comparing with the glory that is to be revealed to us" (Rom. 8:16–18 ESV).

And this powerful poetry:

> But we have this treasure in jars of clay, to show that the surpassing power belongs to God and not to us. We are afflicted in every way, but not crushed; perplexed, but not driven to despair; persecuted, but not forsaken; struck down, but not destroyed; always carrying in the body the death of Jesus, so that the life of Jesus may also be manifested in our bodies . . . So we do not lose heart. Though our outer self is wasting away, our inner self is being renewed day by day. For this light momentary affliction is preparing for us an eternal weight of glory beyond all comparison. (2 Cor. 4:7–10, 16–17 ESV)

There is a great mystery here: somehow our suffering and the very suffering of Christ are related. It seems as if God views them as being one and the same; we are drawn deep within the life of Jesus, and that life is deep within us.

Although Paul had experienced great pain as a direct result of persecution, such as few First World followers of Jesus could claim today, he also knew the more mundane suffering of bodily affliction. A little later in this second letter to the Corinthian church, he relates how "a thorn was given [him] in the flesh." Whatever the affliction actually was, it certainly sounds painful! Strangely, although Paul identified this thorn as "a messenger of Satan," he also clearly understood that it was ultimately given to him from God (2 Cor. 12:7–10 ESV).

When we open our hands to receive the gifts from God that we may find within the pain in our lives or bodies, we, too, are opening ourselves to learn that God's grace is sufficient for us and that his strength is perfected in our weakness. For when we are weak, then we are strong.

Trusting that whatever God chooses to give us, whether pleasurable or painful, his gifts will ultimately be revealed as good and perfect, we pray:

Lord, open my hands,
that I may release what I have held,
and so hold what you give me,
be molded by your touch,
and reach out to others.

Becoming

Lord, open my hands,
that I may release what I have held,
and so hold what you give me,
be molded by your touch,
and reach out to others.

There is an irresistible image drawn for us in the story of creation told in the first chapters of the Bible. The actual text says this:

> This is the account of the heavens and the earth when they were created, when the LORD God made the earth and the heavens.
>
> Now no shrub had yet appeared on the earth and no plant had yet sprung up, for the LORD God had not sent rain on the earth and there was no one to work the ground, but streams came up from the earth and watered the whole surface of the ground. The LORD God formed a man from the dust of the ground and breathed into his nostrils the breath of life, and the man became a living being. (Gen. 2:4–7)

Imagine this:

The sun above is almost white in the heat of its newness, but even its searing rays get distracted and diffused in the mist. They wander earthward, their gilded paths shredded, finally splaying tentative fingers against rock barely cooled and undulating fields of loamy earth. Everywhere there are small geysers and springs burping their way up through black mud, racing off in exuberant streams and rivers or resting in quiet pools.

Here and there, where the sun has fought its way clear of the fog, a light-green bristle shades the slopes, but it's the only sign of life—the only outward sign—yet in the vast silence you can almost hear life itself, feel it humming beneath the dirt.

You wander through the endless morning. The sun gathers its strength; the mist is separated into golden droplets and tempted upward, upward, until it relinquishes itself. In the areas where it is farthest from the pools and running water, the soil begins to dry out: black mud becomes brown dirt, and upon the dirt, in spots, grows a paler lace of dust.

In one such place, you come upon a figure on its knees, fingers plowed deep into the soil. At first it seems the sun is even brighter here, until you notice that this figure radiates its own light, in a kind of pulsing dance with the sunlight, and the hum of life you have been feeling through the soles of your feet provides a harmonic to a still stronger note coming from—yes, coming also from the kneeling figure.

The Creator is on his knees in the dirt of the world he has made. Its soil running across his palms. He is intent, focused on this newest artistry, shaping with his hands a figure that might be a self-portrait. He is quick and sure, yet each handful of dust is patted into place tenderly.

You want to see what this new figure looks like, so you move around to the side. The Creator has molded a person, a person beautiful and whole, and no atom of what he has shaped bears any resemblance to dirt anymore. The figure he has formed from the dust of the ground appears familiar to you, and you bend for a closer look.

It's you. The figure is you, perfectly formed, perfectly at peace. It's you the way you were meant to be, the way you long to be and are not yet. It's you waiting to become.

The Creator catches your eye. He smiles and bends toward you. You can feel his breath on your face. It smells like life . . .

That, of course, is not quite the biblical account. And yet, surely a part of what we are to understand from the story is that God has shaped you and me as directly and intimately and individually as he did Adam and Eve.

As David sang, "You created my inmost being; you knit me together in my mother's womb. I praise you because I am fearfully and wonderfully made" (Ps. 139:13–14).

He has made us, and no one who gives even a passing thought

to the complexity, durability, sensitivity, and flexibility of human beings could argue that he has done so "fearfully and wonderfully."

But he is not done with us yet. God is still shaping us.

In what may be an extended riff on the ancient story of the Creator shaping humanity out of dirt, the prophets Isaiah and Jeremiah repeatedly used the image of a potter shaping a vessel out of clay to describe how God was molding his people. As Jeremiah watched one day, a potter working at his wheel took a pot that was marred and "formed it into another pot, shaping it as seemed best to him" (Jer. 18:4).

This clay was wet and still easily malleable. On another occasion, Jeremiah was instructed by God to break a clay jar in front of a group of Hebrew elders as a demonstration of what would happen to the nation if they didn't turn around. That jar had been fired and was fully set; it was smashed and could not be repaired.

Change is hard for most of us, and we usually can't change ourselves very much. Pain, as we have seen, is often the mediator of change in our deeper lives. The more "set" we are, the more difficult it is.

When we pray, *Lord, open us up to be molded by your hands*, we are seeking to remain soft and malleable so that he can shape us as seems best to him. We are releasing our own expectations about what kind of shape we will ultimately have and are abandoning ourselves into the hands of God, trusting that the shape he has in mind for us will be better than the shape we imagine for ourselves. Even clay that has begun to dry out can be returned to a shapeable consistency— although it may take a drenching and some pounding to get it there!

"It is a fearful thing to fall into the hands of the living God," we are warned by the writer of the letter to the Hebrews (10:31 ESV). He was concerned that his audience was too fully set, too determined to pursue their own course, and that the results of doing so would be disastrous.

But what if, falling into the hands of the living God, we discovered we had fallen into the embrace of a loving father?

Luke's story of the prodigal son tells exactly such a tale. You know it: a young man, full of himself and his plans for life, cashed in on his inheritance and took off for more interesting places than his father's farm. His plans failed spectacularly; finding himself alone, stripped of his dignity and dreams, he shambled reluctantly homeward, rehearsing all the way the speech he would make to the father he had shamed.

But the loving father had been watching for his renegade son. Seeing him approaching from a distance, he ran to meet the embarrassed prodigal. The young man had hoped that his father might perhaps allow him to hire on as a servant, for room and board. Before he could make his pitch, the father instead threw his arms around his child and kissed him.

Within that embrace, the young man began to become, for the first time, the true son of his father.

He had demeaned his father, ruined his relationships, blown his fortune, and screwed up his entire future. It took a pounding, but he finally became willing to allow his father to shape him into what he was always meant to be.

How much better would it be if we simply sought, here and now, to be open to the molding God wants to do in our lives?

As Paul wrote to the Ephesian church, "We are God's handiwork, created in Christ Jesus to do good works, which God prepared in advance for us to do" (Eph. 2:10).

Most English translations, unfortunately, give an uninspiring tone to the intent of the expression, *God's handiwork*. It sounds as if God has made us to be useful, utilitarian, and probably not very imaginative: a bench, maybe, or a simple bookshelf. But the word translated *handiwork* would, rendered into our alphabet, read *poema*.

It's the Greek word from which we get our English word *poem*. While the phrase doesn't literally mean that we are God's poetry—that would be imposing the English meaning upon the Greek—it does remind us that we are his artistry, the deliberate expression of his eternal power and divine nature.[5] And that is an entirely more spacious conception of who we are becoming than anything we might arrive at ourselves.

The greatest gift God places into our hands is the gift of himself. We take bread in our hands and break it. We eat it, and it becomes a part of us. The Holy Spirit dwells within us, and Christ is within us, as we are in him. As he gave his body for us, so we are becoming the body of Christ in the world. He is shaping us, as he sees fit, to become active, expressive members of that body.

Because we want to live into God's vision of what we can become, we pray:

> Lord, open my hands,
> that I may release what I have held,
> and so hold what you give me,
> *be molded by your touch,*
> and reach out to others.

Doing

> Lord, open my hands,
> that I may release what I have held,
> and so hold what you give me,
> be molded by your touch,
> *and reach out to others.*

Think of all the incredible things a pair of hands can do. From surgery to blacksmithing, from playing the violin to prizefighting—the range of two palms, two thumbs, and eight fingers is astonishing. (I have a friend who does amazing things with no fingers or thumbs at all.)

Touching, grasping, holding, stroking, punching, poking, pinching. Throwing and catching. Writing, drawing, gesturing . . .

Think of all the incredible things *your* hands do every day, many without you thinking very much at all: fitting a slender key to the tiny hole in a lock, picking up a sandwich, brushing your teeth. Manipulating a steering wheel, or a blender, or a coffee cup, a wallet, the myriad tools and papers and machinery, large and small, of any working life.

Here is a partial sample of the things my hands have done today by midmorning: made the bed, lifted weights, scrubbed the rest of me in the shower, buttoned my shirt, opened and closed the fridge, made espresso, guided several spoons of yogurt and granola to my mouth, fixed the flat tire on my bike. At this very moment, my fingers are searching out keys on my laptop—without me looking at them or giving them any instruction other than thinking about what the next word will be and how it is spelled.

I realize, looking at this list, that most of what I have done so far today I have done for myself. But we have agreed that this contemplative path is about more than merely our own individual relationships with God—contemplation without action is like faith without works: it's dead. A true contemplative path cannot be a selfish one.

The prophet Hosea used the image of the Old Testament patriarch Jacob in his lifelong struggle with God. This, really, is what a contemplative path is: our lifelong struggle to become more open to God and, through him, to ourselves and to others. After relating how Jacob wrestled and overcame the angel, and later encountered God again at Bethel, Hosea urged the struggler-with-God: "So you, by the help of your God, return, hold fast to love and justice, and wait continually for your God" (Hos. 12:6 ESV).

We, too, are asking God to help us turn our faces toward him. Our seeking to become more open to him, moment by moment, through each day, is a way of "waiting continually" for him. We can't "hold fast to love and justice" for ourselves; they must be offered outward. This means reaching out to others and seeking the best for them. We may, and should, love anyone and everyone; God's kingdom justice is for people who are poor, oppressed, afflicted. Keeping a firm grip on actively loving and seeking justice ought to be how we "do life."

With these things in mind, as we pray, *Lord, open my hands to reach out to others*, let's consider three ways in which we may hold fast to love and justice: giving, touching, and working. (There are an almost infinite number of modes of reaching out that could be considered. You might want to come up with your own, or you may become aware as you walk this stretch of the path that God is opening you up to a very specific kind of reaching out.)

We've looked at Jesus' parable of the sheep and the goats a few times already. Consider it again, and let's ponder this time all the ways the hands of the righteous are involved in giving: "For I was hungry and you gave me food, I was thirsty and you gave me drink, I was a stranger and you welcomed me, I was naked and you clothed me, I was sick and you visited me, I was in prison and you came to me" (Matt. 25:35–36 ESV).

Jesus' words make it clear that reaching out to others is how we are to live out the good news he came to proclaim. It's relatively easy for us to share food and drink and resources with the people close to us—our families and friends. But it can be quite a challenge for us to invite a stranger into this circle.

We may encounter, then, an embarrassing nakedness, a

neediness or degradation we feel unequipped to clothe. We will encounter sicknesses we know we cannot heal. Every prison I have ever visited was an unsettling place merely to enter: darkness and despair lurk in every corner. What have we to give, when separated by a wide gulf of experience, let alone a sheet of bulletproof glass?

And yet, we must reach toward need such as this. We can't just stay within the comfortable circle of our social, economic, or religious peers. Any serious measure of contemplation will confirm in us the inkling that to be members of the human family and to be followers of Jesus, we must share whatever material excess we have with our brothers and sisters who have less. This is exactly what kingdom justice looks like. This is the gospel of Jesus Christ in action.

Still, sharing food and drink with people who are destitute, while simple enough in itself, will quickly reveal to us that we are ultimately reaching out with empty hands. The deepest human needs are not ones that can be satisfied with food or clothing or medicine, but only through the salvation, the deliverance, offered through the Spirit of God. We will quickly arrive at a sense of our insufficiency as givers, *and this is not a bad place to be.*

As we pray, *Lord, open our hands to give,* we are also asking him to fill our hands even as we reach out. Reaching out with empty hands teaches us to trust in God's sufficiency rather than our own. And so, even as we give, God is giving to us.

When we reach out to give to people who are in need, and find that the stuff we have to offer is not, on its own, enough, we will inevitably learn how important it is to touch. In fact, we will begin to realize that people, in their poverty or neediness or even violence, are actually our brothers and sisters. We will find ourselves *wanting* to touch people whom we once found intimidatingly "other."

Among his many miracles, Jesus showed a few times that he

was able to heal people from a distance. But most often, he chose to touch—lifting lame people to their feet, smearing mud on the eyes of a blind man, even reaching out to touch lepers and others whom his contemporaries considered unclean.

There is a whole other level of healing, blessing, affirmation, and empowerment that is possible when we reach out with open hands—without ulterior motive, in an attitude of giving rather than taking—to touch.

We noticed, earlier in the chapter, that the prodigal son began to grow into his true identity at the moment his father embraced him. That's the power of touch.

Henri Nouwen, in his brilliant book *The Return of the Prodigal Son*, relates how, as he spent hours contemplating the Rembrandt painting of the same name, he recognized himself as first the wayward son, and then as the faithful but resentful elder son who stayed home. And finally, Henri realized God was calling him to a new way of being: he was being invited to become the loving father who embraced both sons.[6]

We, too, as we walk homeward along this contemplative path, are being molded more and more fully in the image of the One who made us and is making us. We are being called to become parents whose very touch can welcome into a true home those children who are wayward or faithful, wild or uptight, repentant or resentful.

Such healing power is not within our human grasp. Once again, we reach out what we discover are empty hands to others, trusting that God will fill them. And once again, in the mysterious economy of the kingdom, we will find he not only empowers our touch for the good of others but also blesses us: Jesus promises us that, in touching the untouchable, we are touching him.

When we have given what we can and touched where we are able, we will find there is still work to do.

In the Sermon on the Mount, Jesus said, "In the same way, let your light shine before others, so that they may see your good works and give glory to your Father who is in heaven" (Matt. 5:16 ESV).

What might those good works be? Paul had a lot to say about good works, too, but neither he nor Jesus ever detail exactly what they are: *Here's a list of good works you should do . . .*

Perhaps this means it should be obvious to us what those good works are. Feeding hungry people, giving a drink to someone thirsty—the things we've already looked at are clearly kingdom works. Speaking through the prophet Isaiah, God told the people of Israel,

> *Is not this the kind of fasting I have chosen:*
> *to loose the chains of injustice*
> *and untie the cords of the yoke,*
> *to set the oppressed free*
> *and break every yoke?* (Isa. 58:6)

That's about challenging the powerful, deeply entrenched systems of oppression and injustice that abound in our world. It certainly sounds like work!

Paul also encouraged Timothy to fulfill his calling by doing "the work of an evangelist,"[7] and frequently referred to his own "work" or "labors" in missionary service, as well as his paying gig as a manufacturer of tents. While every follower of Jesus should, in life and especially in deed, be announcing the good news, not all of us are called to be evangelists, and perhaps even fewer to be missionaries or ministers.

I wonder if the reason Jesus and Paul don't bother to list exactly what works we should engage in is because the *kind* of work really doesn't matter all that much. Maybe what matters more is that we simply *do something*—something that requires some effort—to reach out to other people, especially people who are in need. Sometimes we are inclined to show great interest in the spiritual work of others, feeling perhaps that our interest or even prayers are close enough to actually working ourselves. Some of us are inclined to write a check rather than get our own hands dirty; others spend a long time praying for direction about what they should do, effectively sitting on both hands and wallet.

Supporting the work of others with our interest, prayers, and money is a good thing. Praying for God's direction is a good thing too. But the more we pray, *Lord, open my hands to reach out to others*, the more compelled we will be to get out of our chairs (or pews) and also do material work for the good of others.

We can trust that if we reach out with hands open to work for other people, God will guide us, redeem our mistaken efforts, and much more. Jesus promised, "Truly, truly, I say to you, whoever believes in me will also do the works that I do; and greater works than these will he do, because I am going to the Father" (John 14:12 ESV).

Imagine what thoughts would go through our minds if we heard someone claim, "I will do greater works than Jesus." And yet, this is what he promised—not on the basis of our having the proper training, or giving extraordinary effort, or having exemplary physiques or intellects, but simply because we trust him. The value of any work we do will accrue to it because we have dared to reach out open, empty hands, believing that God will direct and empower them.

And that is why we pray:

Lord, open my hands,
that I may release what I have held,
and so hold what you give me,
be molded by your touch,
and reach out to others.

Remember . . .

- We are not likely to be touched or held ourselves, nor to touch or hold others in any fulfilling way, if we approach life with fists clenched.
- Releasing our grip on something may simply mean holding it loosely enough in our hands for God to move it, or remove it, as he sees fit.
- The goodness of God's gifts may not appear immediately.
- We can trust that if we reach out with hands open to work for other people, God will guide us.

For Examen (reflection or discussion)

- Are there things you hang on to that seem to own you more than you own them?
- Is the idea that painful experiences may also be a gift of God difficult to accept?
- Can you identify a pain or sorrow of your own that has turned out to be a blessing?
- How is God molding you at this stage of your life?
- What good work are you doing or could you do for others, especially others who are in need?

7

Open My Mind

Lord, open my mind,
that I may release what I have understood,
and so understand you,
understand myself,
and understand others.

UNDERSTANDING

We've all experienced it. Someone is trying to explain something to us—a news story, how an internal combustion engine works, why a promise wasn't fulfilled—and we just aren't getting it. Somehow, it just doesn't add up. Then the person explaining realizes that she has left out one salient fact; she tosses it into the mix, and comprehension dawns.

"Dawn" is a good analogy. When we finally understand something, it's like the sun has risen over a darkened landscape. The previously shrouded features of the vista before us, and our orientation within it, finally make sense to us. In fact, it looks like dawn on a person's face, doesn't it? The clouded brow, squinting eyes, mouth slightly pursed; then understanding pierces the darkness and the entire face lightens.

Understanding is more than merely knowing. *Knowing*, as we think of the term, is largely about possessing the facts. Facts may be the building blocks of understanding, but there are a great many people who can carry bricks and are nevertheless unable to build a house. Understanding means being able to perceive how those facts fit together, and what the implications of their assembly are.

That makes the matter of understanding sound a little mechanical, a little bloodless. But we know different. When we understand someone's struggles, it moves us away from judgment and toward compassion. When we understand the true nature of a problem, it releases us from despair and helps us determine a course of action. When we understand ourselves, we may be freed from destructive patterns, set loose to laugh at ourselves, and empowered to embrace our true identity in new, creative ways.

Misunderstanding does just the opposite, and history is full of proof. The Crusades and the Inquisition simply can't be rationalized with thoughtful Christian faith by anyone who has the merest understanding of the teachings and especially the example of Jesus; yet both were driven in large part by people who believed they were doing God's work.

I know little of Islam, but people who do tell me that jihadist suicide bombers have a similarly perverted view of their own faith. And frankly, it's a great mystery to me how any follower of Jesus could enthusiastically endorse waging war on another nation or oppose measures that would help lift people out of poverty. Yet both still happen.

During the Second World War, German troops went into battle with *"Gott Mitt Uns"* (God With Us) stamped on their belt buckles. American money still bears the inscription "In God We Trust." The UK sings "God Save the Queen." During the Civil War, Union soldiers sang of seeing God's face in their own nighttime campfires and then marched out to kill their Rebel countrymen by day.

I have seen Him in the watch-fires of a hundred circling camps,
They have builded Him an altar in the evening dews and damps;
I can read His righteous sentence by the dim and flaring lamps:
His day is marching on.
(from "The Battle Hymn of the Republic")

It's not new, of course; one way or another virtually every nation in history (until the rise of communism) has co-opted some version of God to their empire-building purposes.

For a few at the top of the heap, certainly, this has been a matter of cynical manipulation of the power of religious belief. But for most, it seems to me, they have misunderstood the nature of their own faith on a colossal and diabolical scale.

A lack of understanding—especially if one doesn't care to understand—is every bit as destructive in relationships between people, or between individuals and God, as it is between nations. On the other hand, even a glimmer of understanding can be incredibly powerful.

When the apostle Paul expressed his desire "that I may know him and the power of his resurrection, and may share his sufferings, becoming like him in his death" (Phil. 3:10 ESV), he meant more than merely assembling the facts about Jesus, his resurrection, suffering, and death. The word he used that is translated *know* means "to know by experience": to get it, to encompass it, to understand it with his whole self.

And when he went on to admit: "Not that I have already obtained this or am already perfect, but I press on to make it my own, because Christ Jesus has made me his own. Brothers, I do not consider that I have made it my own" (vv. 12–13 ESV), he reminded us that truly understanding is a progressive business: a little here, a little there, slowly pressing on. The Greek word here translated *made it my own* means "to lay hold of so as to possess as one's own." That's what we mean by understanding.

Although we have accumulated a great many facts about the human brain, the means by which it understands remains a mystery in itself. Gottfried von Leibniz, a German philosopher and scientist, expressed this in the eighteenth century by comparing the brain to a windmill. He observed that the working parts of the brain do not themselves explain how it, unlike the mill, actually perceives rather than merely fulfilling a function:

> One is obliged to admit that *perception* and what depends upon it is *inexplicable on mechanical principles*, that is, by figures and motions . . . One should, when visiting within it [an enormously expanded brain], find only parts pushing one another, and never anything by which to explain a perception.[1]

We know more now about what the brain does and what its working parts are; but how exactly it comprehends remains to a large degree a mystery.

Mystery is what understanding pursues. And the greatest mystery of all is God himself. When we embark on a path to understanding God, we know the journey will never end. As we press on, we are humbled more and more by the slow realization of the scope of both our own ignorance and his magnitude. Strangely, this is not discouraging; to the contrary, the greatness of the mystery draws us deeper in. We understand more and more, and exactly how we understand what we understand is, itself, a mystery.

If we say "I understand" and mean thereby "I have already encompassed the matter entirely," we close the door to deeper understanding. When a little light dawns, we must not assume it is all the light there is. We must remain open, wider and wider open, so the light of understanding will flood deeper and deeper into our minds, illuminating the crevices and dark corners that have remained uninspected so long we have forgotten, if we ever knew, that they are there.

This is a bold venture—letting go of preconceived notions, daring to seek to understand God, ourselves, others. It is not a path we can tread alone. So we put our hands into the hand of the Mystery, praying:

Lord, open my mind,
that I may release what I have understood,
and so understand you,
understand myself,
and understand others.

Releasing

Lord, open my mind,
that I may release what I have understood,
and so understand you,
understand myself,
and understand others.

Almost everyone agrees that having an open mind is a good thing, but most of us are reluctant to give up the opinions that keep our minds closed.

Almost all of us feed ourselves regularly on preconceived ideas that are a stew of opinions that are attractive to us; perspectives we've grown up with and have either assimilated or reacted against; facts that are random and often out of context, lightly spiced with a pinch here and there of information we suspect is not really, completely, well . . . true. The current crop of celebrity atheists have with some justification described religious belief in such terms, but are themselves hardly free of the same habit.

We long for certainty because it provides us with an apparently secure foundation for building our lives. We may tend to choose our convictions because they suit how we want to see ourselves or how we want to act, rather than the reverse. Many pastors and counselors have observed that a significant sudden shift in an individual's theological convictions generally coincides with a correlative change in his or her moral behavior.

Our convictions—the things we're sure we understand—anchor us in our individual universes. If someone tries to disprove what we believe, we feel threatened personally, because those beliefs help form our sense of who we are. If our certainties are eroded, we feel disoriented, vulnerable. Choosing to hoist up those anchors, we are afraid, may leave us adrift without a compass or horizon to locate us.

In our relationships with other people, being certain of the rightness of our own point of view makes for argument and polarization rather than open discussion and increasing clarity. Even if we remain in disagreement with each other, we do well to remember (and even admit!) that it's possible, just possible, that we are wrong. Certainty may attract followers of a particular sort, but it does not invite intimate relationship. Only openness does that.

We long for certainty, and yet certainty is the enemy of understanding. Having an open mind means being willing to consider the possibility that what we thought we knew may not be so; curiosity, mystery, and even doubt are much more fertile grounds for deeper understanding. It's only by holding lightly what we think we understand now that we can hope to understand more.

What, then, are we asking for when we pray, *Lord, open our minds to release what we have understood*?

Is it a bad thing to have convictions? Opinions? Should we not seek answers? Is there anything we can be sure of? If we are to let go of our certainties, are we to become skeptics, insisting on the impossibility of knowing anything?

Poor old Job was faced with this problem. At each fresh disaster in his life, another pillar of his understanding of God was knocked away. He grieved his losses, but "did not sin by charging God with wrongdoing" (Job 1:22). Essentially, this means that while he didn't understand what was going on, he continued to trust in the character of God.

"Shall we accept good from God, and not trouble?" (2:10), he said to his understandably angry, distraught wife when she challenged his faith.

Nevertheless, he cursed the very day he had been born—in remarkably elaborate terms too! The man who had been sure God would protect him because he was morally upright, fair with his workers, generous to the poor, kind to his enemies, and honest about his own failings discovered that his relationship with his Maker was not on a fee-for-service basis.

His three "friends" came around to try to explain to him where he'd gone wrong and just how this God thing worked. They were very sure of themselves, sure they had it right. But Job knew their dogmatic views did not match his situation. He responded with bitter sarcasm to their certainty—the same certainty he once held himself:

Doubtless you are the only people who matter,
and wisdom will die with you!
But I have a mind as well as you;
I am not inferior to you.
Who does not know all these things? (12:2–3)

The longer the argument went on, the more virulent Job's speech became. He was angry, anguished, and utterly confused about what was happening to him and why. In stronger and stronger terms, he accused God of treating him unjustly. He ached to be able to return to the way things used to be, when his universe was unfolding as he understood it was supposed to:

How I long for the months gone by,
for the days when God watched over me,
when his lamp shone on my head
and by his light I walked through darkness . . .

I thought, "I will die in my own house,
my days as numerous as the grains of sand.
My roots will reach to the water,
and the dew will lie all night on my branches."
(29:2–3, 18–19)

When Job finally ran out of vitriol, a young man named Elihu (whose name means "He is my God"), who had been listening to the conversation, could contain himself no longer.

Launching into a lengthy speech of his own, Elihu did not, like the other friends, accuse Job of some hidden, heinous sin. At the most, he chided the older man for self-righteousness. Instead, he reflected on God's infinite nature, his justice and mercy. His own understanding of who God is and how he relates to humanity came not from age or other conventional human sources of wisdom, but "it is the spirit in a person, the breath of the Almighty, that gives them understanding" (32:8).

Elihu concluded with this powerful image of the God with whom Job was wrestling:

> *Out of the north he comes in golden splendor;*
> *God comes in awesome majesty.*
> *The Almighty is beyond our reach and exalted in power;*
> *in his justice and great righteousness, he does not oppress.*
> (37:22–23)

If this is so, is it any wonder we must learn to loosen our grip on the things we think we understand about the God we seek? Ultimately, Job did exactly that. After God had finally spoken—without a word of apology for the extraordinary trials he had allowed the poor man to endure, but with a blistering poetic rant about his unfathomable creative power—Job finally let go.

He let go of his understanding of himself as being deserving of all the good things he had once had and undeserving of his tribulations. He let go of his understanding of God as a kind of celestial customer service department and acknowledged his framework of understanding was founded on irrelevancies. "Surely," he said, "I spoke of things I did not understand, things too wonderful for me to know" (42:3).

And, by the way, those three friends who were so certain they had God and Job nailed? God threatened their very lives for lying about him if they did not beg Job to make sacrifices on their behalf.

When I was in my late teens, I began to notice cracks in the seemingly impenetrable theological dogma with which I had grown up. At first, being young and also by nature somewhat iconoclastic, it was exciting to think that things might be other than I had been taught. But when my enthusiasm—for what, to me, were new ways of understanding God and the church—was met with concern, then anger, and finally rejection, I found it disorienting and even frightening to be without the old foundation of "the things most assuredly believed among us."

I found that, having opened a gap for one or two uncertainties, others thrust their way in behind them. The gap widened until it seemed I was in danger of being trampled beneath a stampeding herd. I worried that I was losing track of who God was and how I was supposed to follow him. I worried that I was losing track of myself! I feared the damage or even outright loss of many of the relationships that were dearest to me.

Every one of my worries and fears came to pass.

But, despite my losses, there was no way back. Having let go of the things I thought I understood, I discovered I could not pick them up again—at least, not in the same way. For much of what I had been convinced had been revealed as suspect, or even untrue. To go back was to commit a kind of spiritual and intellectual suicide. Some of the things I had understood previously survived the stampede, but even they appeared different; my perspective had been skewed. And never again could I be as certain of anything as I had been before.

It feels, at times, as if my entire adult life has been one continuous process of having stripped away from me the certainties on which I once relied.

Here's the curious thing: the more I have come to know God experientially—the way Paul spoke of knowing the power of resurrection—the less I'm sure I really understand *about* God factually. To put it another way, the more I loosen my grip on my restrictive understanding about God, the bigger, fuller, wilder, more loving and gracious he seems to become. There is tremendous freedom in this. The more we open our minds, the more he fills them up. It's like cleaning the junk out of a disused room so that it can become a space for living.

This is what we're seeking, isn't it? More space in our busy lives to live with God? So then, as unnerving as it may be to do so, we pray:

Lord, open my mind,
that I may release what I have understood,
and so understand you,
understand myself,
and understand others.

Receiving

Lord, open my mind,
that I may release what I have understood,
and so understand you,
understand myself,
and understand others.

Lord, open our minds, so that we may understand *you.*

This, it seems to me, is an audacious prayer. For not only must we release our preconceptions of who God is, but we must also admit that, really, God can never be understood by us—not fully. He is too big, and we are too little. Does a child really understand the complexity of his parents' lives?

As Augustine so cogently expressed it, "If you understood him, he would not be God."[2] That's the essential point of God's long speech at the end of the book of Job.

Why, then, do we ask to understand him? And what do we mean by *understand* when we ask?

The good news, the truly good news, is that God wants to be known. Nature itself is a constant witness to his immediacy and accessibility. The biblical story in its entirety is evidence of this, and a great many of the stories within it express God's desire for us to seek him and understand what we can of him. And clearest of all is the story of Jesus, the Word who came to express the "unknowable" nature of God.

The problem we face is not that God hides himself, for he doesn't. It's simply a problem of scale: it would be easier for me to wrap my arms around a city block than to encompass infinity with my mind.

But this is not a reason to stop seeking a wider and deeper understanding of God any more than the scale of the universe should compel astronomers to pack up their telescopes, or the breadth and depth of the ocean should set marine biologists ashore discouraged and despondent. A part of the excitement for scientists—and for seekers of God—is the knowledge that the journey of discovery is never-ending.

Richard Dawkins, the evolutionary biologist and noted apologist for atheism, has been quoted as saying, "I am against religion because it teaches us to be satisfied with not understanding the world."[3] He may have a point, if by religion he means the human systems that—like economics, politics, and militarism—have been developed and used to control people.

But God actually wants us to seek to understand him, and his creation, better: *seek and you will find* is a refrain that begins with the Mosaic law, continues through the prophets, and is expanded upon by Jesus and the New Testament authors.

The speech God made to Job, the one that completely reordered Job's understanding of himself, his Maker, and his world, is in large part a panegyric to the wonders of creation. Early on, just as he was getting nicely warmed up, God asked rhetorically, "Who has put wisdom in the inward parts or given understanding to the mind?" (Job 38:36 ESV).

"I've given you the tools," God said, in effect. "Do you actually want to begin to understand a little about me, instead of insisting on stuffing me into your premade, miniscule, intellectual-theological-cultural box? Why not start by wondering at and wondering about the world around you? After all, I made it."

As Albert Einstein said, "I want to know how God created this world. I am not interested in this or that phenomenon, in the spectrum of this or that element. I want to know his thoughts. The rest are details."[4] Although Einstein described himself as a "deeply religious non-believer"[5] and did not conceive of God as a personality, he repeatedly cast his research in terms of a spiritual quest, as did his great scientific hero, Sir Isaac Newton:

> This most beautiful system of the sun, planets and comets, could only proceed from the counsel and dominion of an intelligent and powerful Being . . . Blind metaphysical necessity, which is certainly the same always and everywhere, could produce no variety of things. All that diversity of natural things which we find suited to different times and places could arise from nothing but the ideas and will of a Being necessarily existing.[6]

And so, in asking God to open our minds to understand him better, we ought to (in Einstein's phrase) never lose our "holy curiosity"[7] about our universe and its Creator. For Newton and Einstein, scientific and spiritual curiosity were indivisible.

That Christians believe the Bible to be the Word of God—that God has invested his Spirit in a volume of written words we can pick up at any time—is a reminder we do not worship one who holds himself at a distance; we worship one who makes himself near and accessible. The sacred scriptures of any faith bear witness to the same human instinct that the Creator desires to be known and understood.

Many stories within the Bible underscore that belief. The creation story reminds us that we are surrounded by the evidence of God's creative energies; that each and every human being we encounter is a fresh revelation of the One in whose image he or she is made. The accounts in Genesis and Exodus of his relationships with the patriarchs and the emerging nation of Israel reveal a God who is so eager to be understood that he not only converses with and delivers specific instructions to his people but also is willing to go on the road with them. In the prophetic books, it's not God who's disinterested—it's the people who keep turning away, and he keeps pleading for them to turn back and seek him once more.

But for the follower of Jesus, the most potent proof of God's desire to be understood is Jesus himself. In his gospel, John calls him "the Word": the articulation of the otherwise unknowable Thought that is God. The Greek term *logos*, from which we get our English word *logic*, also infers balance—all things in proper relationship within the cosmos. In his first letter, the same apostle lists some of the ways Jesus offered himself as a means of knowing God: "That which was from the beginning, which we have heard, which we have seen with our eyes, which we have looked at and our hands have touched—this we proclaim concerning the Word of life" (1 John 1:1).

This Word—this embodiment and expression of the almighty God, who took on human flesh and lived and died among and for us—by each action and every uttered phrase leads us to a deeper understanding of the Great Mystery.

Mystery is not forbidding. Every mystery is an invitation to press deeper in. We know that in doing so our preconceptions will be challenged and often dismantled. New vistas of understanding will unfold before us.

In nature, we may press deeper in by rigorous scientific investigation or merely by casual observation; often the former is prompted by the latter. Remember the tale of the apple falling on Isaac Newton's head and his subsequent lifelong fascination with the properties of gravity? I am no scientist, but I know that golden autumn leaves drifting through pale sunlight to carpet the ground beneath my feet reveal something to me about the character of God, if I am open to receive it.

Let's face it: understanding the Bible really well is about as easy as mastering quantum physics. A lifetime of intensive theological study is apparently not enough, as so many who have thus devoted themselves are in such disagreement with one another. But contemplation is not a science, nor is it a subject to be mastered. Anyone—even you and I—may read Scripture or hear it read and, holding it lightly, discern something fresh about the God who breathes within it. We have been doing so throughout these chapters.

Understanding Jesus better is best done by simply following him. By this we mean trying to be obedient to his teachings, as far as we understand them (the disciples by no means understood them perfectly!), and trying to be like him as far as we are able. While this isn't very complicated, it also isn't easy. To do either immaculately, let alone both, is as far beyond our powers as complete comprehension of the mystery of God. But that simply doesn't matter. Understanding God is not a war to be won, nor a deal to be closed. It's a path along which we walk day by day.

Many years ago, I lay on a dock and watched the aurora borealis—the Northern Lights—dance around the deep velvet bowl of the midnight sky. Arcs of bright pale-blue and green cascaded from its apogee, shivering as they streamed down toward the treetops, black and ragged, that rimmed the lake. Their reflections scorched a cold, wriggling trail across the still water in counterpoint to the evolutions above. These limbs of light shifted through sequence after sequence of changement in wild yet perfectly sympathetic synchronicity, tracing their movements across the vault. They melted, then they shook and shimmied like a woman in her finest clothes balling the jack in some glorious juke joint in the Delta.

Somewhere, I'm sure, far beyond my human hearing, a band of celestial musicians played their hearts out. I was at once humbled and exalted.

When we encounter something—or Someone—that is too great for us to encompass with our understanding, it ought to bring us to wonder. Wonder in two ways: first, in the sense of wondering *at* it—the experience of awe. And second, in the sense of wondering *about* it. *I wonder . . .* which is the beginning of inquiry; the question by which we begin pressing deeper into the ineffable mystery.

Perhaps you have noticed that as we have talked about understanding God and thought a little about some ways we might begin to do so, we have said nothing about the kinds of new understanding we might gain.

That's because we don't know! We want to be open to whatever it is he chooses to reveal about himself. The possibilities are infinite. That's why we pray:

Lord, open my mind,
that I may release what I have understood,
and so understand you,
understand myself,
and understand others.

Becoming

Lord, open my mind,
that I may release what I have understood,
and so understand you,
understand myself,
and understand others.

"There are three Things extremely hard," Benjamin Franklin said. "Steel, a Diamond and to know one's self."[8]

We spend years in school, mastering a variety of subjects, and thousands of hours of work and leisure time over the course of years learning to sell, build, keep the books, fix things, play sports, ride motorcycles, knit, bake, and much more. Every new project comes with a learning curve; and with many, the curve may flatten out a little with time but never really lose its arc. The activities of others intrigue us too: we pore over Facebook postings or read articles and books about celebrities, fascinated by what makes other people tick.

But we spend surprisingly little time trying to understand ourselves. Most of us approach the world expecting it to understand us, whether we understand ourselves or not.

There's a difference between knowing about and truly knowing, or understanding, oneself. I have dozens of friends, for instance, who know they are addicts, and may even know their addictions are empowered by abuses they suffered as children—but they are powerless to change the patterns and choices that are slowly killing them.

The circumstances of my addicted friends throw their lack of self-understanding into sharp relief, but they are certainly not alone. How many people whose success reveals their tremendous understanding of the business world possess so little self-knowledge that they alienate their own families? I know a formerly prominent and highly effective psychiatrist who drank himself out of his practice and is now drinking himself to death. I know a number of former ministers and preachers who have blown their lives out of the water, surprising everyone, including themselves, by embarking on affairs, often of the most ridiculous and unprincipled sort. These actions are not prompted by a good understanding of oneself!

When I look back on the more cataclysmic events of my own life, some of them many years ago now, I still find myself wondering what happened and how my own behaviors contributed to the mess. Furthermore, there are a host of smaller ways in which I make decisions day by day that I know to be less than excellent; I know it in the very moment that I am deciding—but that doesn't stop me.

Do you relate to this? Take heart. So did the apostle Paul.

> I do not understand my own actions. For I do not do what I want, but I do the very thing I hate . . . For I know that nothing good dwells in me, that is, in my flesh. For I have the desire to do what is right, but not the ability to carry it out. For I do not do the good I want, but the evil I do not want is what I keep on doing . . . Wretched man that I am! Who will deliver me from this body of death? (Rom. 7:15, 18–19, 24 ESV)

No wonder we avoid self-inspection. Any remotely honest appraisal will reveal that we are not nearly as strong, thoughtful, altruistic, honest—we are just not as *good* as we'd like to believe ourselves to be. It's much easier, and more pleasant, to accept the family dog's unfailing admiration as a true measure of our splendid character.

Self-knowledge can be so overwhelming and discouraging that C. S. Lewis admitted he often prayed for only "the little daily dose" that he thought he'd be able to manage.[9] But knowing the awful, darkling truth about ourselves is not really the goal.

And, it must be said, neither have we reached the goal if what we discover about ourselves is that we are much further ahead, more skilled, more attractive, more intelligent than we had thought. What a gift to come to such a realization! But there's more.

We don't want to drown in depression because of our faults, but neither do we want to become infatuated with ourselves because of our graces. We pray for openness so that, with the clear understanding of who we are, we may find and claim our true selves—the selves that God, with complete knowledge of both our brokenness and beauty, has granted us, and which he values above anything else in his creation.

God has no intention of erasing our faults, nor does he intend to pay attention only to our better qualities. He intends to transfigure both.

A few chapters after moaning about his unlovely moral state, Paul reflected on God's faithfulness and his greatness, and so encouraged the Roman disciples to offer themselves as living sacrifices to God. He went on: "Do not be conformed to this world, but be transformed by the renewal of your mind, that by testing you may discern what is the will of God, what is good and acceptable and perfect" (Rom. 12:2 ESV).

The word *transformed* here is the same as that translated *transfigured* in Matthew 17:2—the account of the revelation of Jesus as the Son of God and the fulfillment of the Law and Prophets on a mountaintop before Peter, James, and John. Although both are good translations, I prefer the word *transfigured*. It reminds us that the process of transformation is aimed at taking everything we are, here and now—the good, the bad, the ugly, the beautiful; very rarely are we purely one or the other—and reshaping us into our true beings, our unique selves. These selves will glow with the glory of the One who made us in his image, embraced and affirmed as beloved Sons and Daughters of the Eternal Father.

Our English word *metamorphosis* comes from the Greek word used here for *transformed*, and gives some sense of what is being described: the change of an outer form as the result of inward change. The *renewal* of the mind by which the transformation is to be effected means almost the same thing: a continuing process of being renovated by an inward reformation.

Both transfiguration and renewal are expressed as imperatives: *be* transformed. We are to undertake deliberate actions that will lead to an increased capability of *discerning* (identifying and understanding) God's good, acceptable, and perfect will for us.

I believe this contemplative path we are exploring together is one such deliberate action. We are choosing, through the course of each day, to make ourselves open to the transfiguring power of God. We ought to expect that, over time, we will be changed, and both our capacity and desire to know God, ourselves, and others will deepen.

If this transfiguration is about choosing to think, act, and so look more like Jesus, how might we begin?

Once again, the apostle Paul had some helpful and very challenging words:

Have this mind among yourselves, which is yours in Christ Jesus, who, though he was in the form of God, did not count equality with God a thing to be grasped, but emptied himself, by taking the form of a servant, being born in the likeness of men. And being found in human form, he humbled himself by becoming obedient to the point of death, even death on a cross. Therefore God has highly exalted him and bestowed on him the name that is above every name, so that at the name of Jesus every knee should bow, in heaven and on earth and under the earth, and every tongue confess that Jesus Christ is Lord, to the glory of God the Father. (Phil. 2:5–11 ESV)

It's thought that this passage was a catechism of the early church—a core teaching learned by heart and recited by individuals and groups who, as yet, had no New Testament scriptures from which they might learn the story of Jesus. Undoubtedly, many first- and second-century Christians rehearsed this poem as the subject of their own contemplation.

And if you considered it at any length, turning over in your mind day by day the phrases that express such extravagant mystery, such reckless expenditure of self, how could you not come to love this Jesus?

But Paul's intent here was primarily to engage the mind, not emotions. Specifically, he wanted to engage the deliberate, thoughtful, self-aware intention of his readers to become more like Jesus—to understand themselves in those terms.

There is nothing that can more quickly reveal the depth of our self-interest than trying to live out the mind of Christ. We already know that we are not *in very nature God*; we discover immediately that we are inclined to cling tenaciously to anything—almost anything at all!—we have identified as ours. We are less than keen, most of us, to diminish ourselves in any way. (Those who do readily abase themselves are often poor, damaged souls acting out of a perverse sense of unworthiness; quite the opposite of Jesus.) Some of us, and here I raise my hand, have a problem with basic obedience, let alone obedience unto death.

Yes, trying to be like Jesus helps us understand ourselves in ways that are not very flattering.

I'm glad, then, that Paul reproduced the entire catechistic poem. Because, although we are not *in very nature God*, we are certainly made in his image, with all the dignity and inherent preciousness that such a heritage confers. And although our attempts to follow Jesus on his path of what Henri Nouwen called "downward mobility" may be pallid at best, Jesus is taking us with him to a place of exaltation. He is lifting us up even now; we, too, will be given new names to go with a redeemed character, and we will share with him the glory of the eternal home.

This, too, is the mind of Christ that ought to be in us. Humility and exaltation are intrinsically linked. Having been humbled by the recognition of our venality, selfishness, and fearfulness, we are in a good position to begin to understand ourselves also as glorious, eternal creatures, transfigured so that we might be filled with the joy of God. "Surely, an humble husbandman that serveth God," said Thomas à Kempis, "is better than a proud philosopher that neglecting himself laboureth to understand the course of the heavens."[10]

We approach truly understanding ourselves in fear of what we suspect we will find, because we understand a little of God and his grace, we are also aware of a slowly building excitement at the possibility we may come to an understanding of ourselves that is far greater than what we could have imagined.

In fear and hope, we pray:

Lord, open my mind,
that I may release what I have understood,
and so understand you,
understand myself,
and understand others.

Doing

Lord, open my mind,
that I may release what I have understood,
and so understand you,
understand myself,
and understand others.

Gary Larsen, creator of the brilliant *The Far Side* comics, once produced a panel that was filled almost entirely with a waddle of penguins, bordered in the distance by ice cliffs. Way back in the crowd, one lone bird with wings upraised was singing, "I gotta be me. Oh, I just gotta be me . . ."

Larsen's funny riff on the ubiquitous human desire to be individuated, to be known as unique—all the while remaining firmly within the group—was totally misunderstood by the original publishers of the cartoon. Larsen had drawn the strip entirely in black and white, and all the penguins looked exactly the same. The publishers so didn't get it that they colored the singer yellow, to make him stand out.

Søren Kierkegaard, the Danish theologian who coined the term *leap of faith* and is considered by some to be the first existential philosopher, was known to complain, "People understand me so little that they do not even understand my laments over their not understanding me!"[11]

Understanding others without first having some understanding of ourselves is impossible. That's why, on this section of the path as in every other, we have focused first on opening ourselves—in this instance to better understand ourselves in the light of a better understanding of God.

Still, we try. Members of helping professions—including me and my justice-oriented activist colleagues—are famously prone to "fixing" others as a means of avoiding dealing with their own deficiencies, just as entrepreneurs may lose themselves in developing a business, or artists in creating their next masterpiece.

But neither are we meant to live, nor to understand, in isolation. If we are gifted with a better understanding of God and ourselves, the gift is almost always delivered to us through the agency of others. It is given so that we ourselves may also become gifts to the people around us.

When King Solomon was newly crowned, God appeared to him in a dream and invited him to ask for whatever he wanted. Solomon's wise response was this: "Give your servant therefore an understanding mind to govern your people, that I may discern between good and evil, for who is able to govern this your great people?" (1 Kings 3:9 ESV).

Solomon instinctively understood that the gift God offered was not only, and not even primarily, for him. The gift, properly received, was *through* him, to the people. Understanding his people and their needs would serve an entire nation—and in unsought consequence, make Solomon the wisest, richest, most powerful, and widely honored ruler in Israel's history.

Although seeking to really understand others will make us a little wiser, it's not likely to make most of us any richer or more powerful if we put that understanding to serving others. Some "understand" others only for the purpose of manipulating them; this may make them rich and powerful, but it certainly doesn't make them wise.

The young king's desire was to know how to do the right thing for his people; he wanted to know how to enact God's justice. Much later in his life, he would write, "Evil men do not understand justice, but those who seek the LORD understand it completely" (Prov. 28:5 ESV).

Understanding justice means understanding what is good and right for others, especially for those who are oppressed, afflicted, vulnerable, or destitute. And understanding that means coming to understand them.

When we consider the great ills of the world around us, we may be reluctant to invest the energy required to really understand the needs of others. How can we ever claim to understand a mother who is so malnourished that she is unable to nurse the child who lies dying in her arms? Or an eleven-year-old girl who sits cross-legged in a sweatshop, picking at stitches for twelve hours each day so that, half a world away, you and I can get the best possible price on a new shirt?

Or, closer to home, how can we understand the ones who throng our wealthy cities, hands and hats outstretched, seeking money for a bite to eat or a few minutes of escape from their pain? The woman in the next office who is always so cranky? The man on the bus who is from another country and doesn't speak English? The couple down the street whose fights can be heard from the sidewalk?

Jesus did it by getting close to us. Consider these remarkable phrases from the letter to the Hebrews:

"Since the children have flesh and blood, he too shared in their humanity" (2:14).

"For this reason he had to be made like them, fully human in every way" (2:17).

"Because he himself suffered when he was tempted, he is able to help those who are being tempted" (2:18).

"Son though he was, he *learned* obedience from what he suffered" (5:8, emphasis added).

The implication is that, as God, he couldn't have really understood us, and we couldn't have believed he understood us, unless he became one of us. How remarkable the statement that God Incarnate had anything at all to learn! But by suffering with us, he came to understand us far better than we understand ourselves— so much so that, as he hung dying between heaven and earth, he could plead our case: "Father, forgive them, for they do not know what they are doing" (Luke 23:34).

Of course, we don't plan to get ourselves crucified. Nor would it help to starve ourselves along with that tragic mother, squat beside the young seamstress day after day, or try to sleep through cold winter nights in a cardboard box beneath a bridge, as some of my friends do.

There is, however, another story from the life of Jesus that we might find ways to emulate. Do you remember how, on the night before he was taken to be crucified, Jesus washed the feet of his disciples? They were shocked: the Master never ought to wash the disciples' feet! Peter even tried to avoid it. But when Jesus had persuaded him, and the job was done, he said to the mystified group, "Do you understand what I have done to you? You call me Teacher and Lord, and you are right, for so I am. If I then, your Lord and Teacher, have washed your feet, you also ought to wash one another's feet . . . If you know these things, blessed are you if you do them" (John 13:12–14, 17 ESV).

It's impossible to wash someone's feet from a distance. It's difficult to wash the feet of a stranger, at least in the sense that Jesus did it. A little later that same evening, Jesus remarked that he no longer thought of the disciples as his servants but as his friends. He had come to know those men intimately; he understood they would need his example of being a servant so that, in the years to come, they would remember how the gospel is rooted in sacrifice, not the exercise of power.

So, coming to understand others as Jesus understood his disciples requires that we get close to people, and that we be willing to set aside position, power, and pride. We should be able to manage this. Not, of course, with the complete abandonment (nor the saving power) we see in Jesus. He was able because he knew utterly who he was. We must admit that our capacity to understand others is subject to our ability to understand ourselves—and that's a significant limitation for most of us!

Understanding others is not all sweetness and light. Even Jesus was often frustrated by the blockheadedness of his disciples. The better we know someone, the more we are able to identify his or her foibles, but that doesn't necessarily mean we will be at ease with them. Sometimes, it's just the opposite: another's familiar quirk can seem like a finger repeatedly poking a bruise. Yet, as Carl Jung noted, "Everything that irritates us about others can lead us to an understanding of ourselves."[12] The faults we readily identify and decry in others may even be a mirror image of our own.

Still, truly understanding each other may be the greatest and most rewarding of human endeavors. If we can remember that each person is a unique and beloved expression of the infinitely creative mind of God, we might also find that each step of understanding her or him better is a step deeper into the Great Mystery himself.

Because we want to open ourselves wide to such a thrilling possibility, we pray:

Lord, open my mind,
that I may release what I have understood,
and so understand you,
understand myself,
and understand others.

Remember . . .

- *Understanding is more than merely knowing.*
- *We long for certainty, yet certainty is the enemy of understanding.*
- *The good news, the truly good news, is that God wants to be known.*

- We pray for openness so that, with the clear understanding of who we are, we may find and claim our true selves.

- Understanding others often helps us understand ourselves–and vice versa!

For Examen (reflection or discussion)

- Is it a challenge to accept that some "certainties" you have held on to could keep you from deeper relationship with God?

- Does it entice you or put you off to think there is no end to the mystery that is God?

- What conception of yourself do you cling to that perhaps keeps you from really understanding yourself as God does?

- What do you find most challenging about getting close to people who are oppressed, destitute, vulnerable, or afflicted? How might you overcome that challenge?

8

Open My Heart

Lord, open my heart,
that I may release what I have loved,
and so receive your love for me,
love you more deeply,
and truly love others.

LOVING

We must teach our hearts to listen to our bodies and minds, for almost always, for good or ill, our hearts command.

Our minds receive and translate the signals our senses send; our hearts interpret what our minds have perceived, granting those perceptions meaning and power in our lives. Joy, fear, longing, satisfaction, delight, disappointment, anger, tenderness, compassion—the whole wide range of human emotions, which at times may be so subtly and curiously mixed that we hardly know what to name them. There is hardly any emotion that is not, to some greater or lesser degree, alloyed with another or others.

And beyond emotion is that broad, often murky area we may call "feelings." Barely conscious we are doing so, we sort innumerable facts, observations, and intuitions; filter them through the experiences and biases that shape our individual points of view; and arrive at opinions, perspectives, or even convictions firmly held.

Emotions and feelings, for the most part, direct our choices and actions, even when we think we are being totally rational. They dictate our choice of mates and careers; the kind of dwellings we will live in, where they are, and how we decorate them; how we relate to the people around us; the color of shoes and style of clothing we choose; the books we read, the movies we watch, and the music we listen to. It may be difficult to define precisely what we mean by our "hearts," but there's no question of the power they wield in our lives.

A heart that does not listen to the measured tones of the mind or the quiet voice of the body is a heart that has run amok. It will certainly do great damage to itself and the people around it—especially to those it loves and by whom it is loved. This is the path of selfishness, addiction, abuse: the extremes of lunatic self-aggrandizement or tragic self-degradation. This is a soul on fire, and it will often scorch others before rendering itself to bitter ash.

The heart must listen, but still it must command, for a heart that is utterly subject to the narrower logic of the mind or the voluptuousness of the body is one that denies its unique and precious self, and separates that self from the Love that shaped it. A heart that abdicates command lies within a soul dying, crushed beneath the expectations of others, beneath unattainable goals, and devoured by appetites that can never be sated.

"Were not our hearts burning within us while he talked with us on the road?" said the two who unknowingly walked the Emmaus road with Jesus, after he had been revealed to them.[1] Their hearts knew what their minds could not deduce.

The heart has ways of knowing that the mind cannot compute. The mind collates and interprets facts; while not dismissing those facts, the heart moves beyond them, carrying doubt with it, to understand the mystery of faith. The mind assesses the current realities; the heart looks further, accepting that which is not yet known or understood, defeating fear and rising in hope. The mind tabulates, renders the accounts; the heart knows there are higher values than those that may be calculated and invests itself in love.

Faith, hope, and love. But the greatest of these is love.[2]

Love is the supreme emotion, the supreme thought, the supreme act: for true love is never merely a feeling but is also a choice of will, and cannot be clutched to oneself like some mere bauble. Love must give issue to action—even if that action is a chosen passivity. Such radical passivity—such passion—is called sacrifice. Sacrifice is the noblest issue of love; any love worthy of the name is hardly possible without it.

Loving another without loving oneself is not love at all. Loving oneself without loving another is an impossibility. We are all connected; we all belong to one another. To love ourselves and others as ourselves is to love God, who made us all; the one who says he loves God without loving his brother is a liar.[3]

Loving is never an ill or a mistake. Only, sometimes, failing to love that which is greater makes a mockery of our love: loving our own nation more than humanity, or loving ourselves more than God or our families, or loving our idealized version of a person instead of the real, flawed human being. A love that is held to oneself, or to one's narrow circle of intimately beloved ones, is a love that will calcify, hardening over time into a knot of mean self-interest. But a love that opens its arms, including instead of excluding, will find its resource deepening and expanding; it will become both stronger and more tender. Love is an inexhaustible supply.

We may describe love, but who can define it? It is the greatest power in the cosmos, as infinitely rich as the One who is himself Love. This is why we ascribe love to the "heart," a mythical organ whose only similarity to the beating muscle in our chest is that it lodges somewhere deep within, and through it courses a mythical fluid that sustains our souls as surely as blood does our bodies. Love may be powerful even in the weakest of minds, the frailest of bodies.

God does not see, hear, inhale, taste, or touch by such limited means as we do. Our senses at their most vital provide only pale metaphors of his abundance, and the initial means by which, dimly, we may begin to know his presence and person. It is in our minds and hearts that we are most like him, for that is where we choose. God is love, and this is why we, his children, long to love and be loved. It's our family heritage. It is the fulfillment of who he made us to be.

Love is the strength by which we become vulnerable, the vulnerability by which we become strong. Love is the great calling of the Eternal Father, the great commandment of the Son of his love. Love is the whispered invitation and proclamation of the Spirit within us. Love is the destination, and loving is the means of getting there.

Loving is the ultimate openness.

That is why we pray:

Lord, open my heart,
that I may release what I have loved,
and so receive your love for me,
love you more deeply,
and truly love others.

Releasing

Lord, open my heart,
that I may release what I have loved,
and so receive your love for me,
love you more deeply,
and truly love others.

You must have heard the saying, "If you love something, let it go. If it comes back to you, it's yours. If it doesn't, it never was."

Every time I hear that, there is a question that rolls reflexively around my mind: *So, if it does come back to me—can I grab it by the throat with both hands and hang on tight?*

I suppose that reaction speaks to my instinctive desire to cling to the people and things that I love. I imagine myself clutching the Beloved Thing—in my mind, it looks like a fat and fluffy bird—and slowly, slowly opening my hands. The BT takes flight: my heart plunges down a dry, constricting throat, passes through an anxiously boiling stomach, and lodges queasily somewhere among my bowels. I would love to be serenely open to the possibility of losing the BT; I would love to be able to rest in knowing that if it continues to fly in ever widening circles until it is lost from sight, it was never really mine anyway.

So, theoretically, no loss. I'm better off without it, and it without me. *Fly, little bird. Be free, and God bless you.*

But it doesn't seem to work like that, at least not for me. That BT might be better off without my smothering "love," but to be really honest, I'd rather hang on to it anyway. My love, in such circumstances, is essentially selfish—more interested in the pleasure I receive than in seeking the good of the Beloved Thing.

Releasing the people and things I love requires a lot of energy, tremendous intentionality, and no little amount of courage. Frankly,

I usually have to be forced to it, resentful and fearful. Perhaps that's why it's so difficult—maybe it would be easier if I chose to let go. I doubt very much that I'm unusual in this.

Love, in our world, frequently looks a lot like ownership. Love, as we practice it, too often dominates that which is loved rather than setting it free, demands a return rather than willingly sacrificing.

Physically abusive relationships are only one extreme of the continuum of *codependency*—how psychologists term relationships in which the individuals involved are unable to release each other or themselves from a form of love that is mutually destructive. Some of us are mothers who struggle to let our kids go as they grow; some of us are husbands who dominate and denigrate our wives in more subtle ways; others may cling to a friend by being needy.

Truly loving, loving enough to let go of that which is beloved, feels incredibly risky. Because it is. In opening up our hearts to release what we love, we become tremendously vulnerable. We must face the very real possibility of losing something or someone who occupies precious space in our tender hearts.

God himself has taken what looks to us like an unreasonable risk, and he continues to make himself open to the possibility of rejection by each and every one of us, each and every day. There can be no doubt of his love for us: "This is how God showed his love among us: He sent his one and only Son into the world that we might live through him" (1 John 4:9).

And Jesus did not obey only because he loved the Father. John tells us that his willing self-sacrifice is the ultimate exemplar of love: "This is how we know what love is: Jesus Christ laid down his life for us" (1 John 3:16).

Consider, for a moment or two, the incredible "gamble" God took. He put it all on the line—and then insisted, continues to insist, that we shallow, self-involved, unimaginative, thoughtless people must freely choose to return his extravagant love. Or not. He will not force us or bind us to him against our will. He knows most of us will not love him and that even those of us who do will only manage a tepid, sporadic, and subjective version of his great passion.

We may diminish this by asserting that our characterization of God as one who would or even could be hurt by our disregard—in the same petty manner that we ourselves would be if someone we loved rejected us—is to diminish his god-ness and saddle him with our own meagerness. We may say God took no risk at all, since he knew beforehand who would or would not say yes to him.

But this is a God who *is* love. The mystery of God and his profligate love for humanity is greater than our tidy, rational equations—great enough to admit paradox. Love by its very nature seeks an unforced, willing reciprocity. It cannot remain unmoved by rejection or indifference, nor by the longed-for return of love. The Lover, by loving, makes himself vulnerable to the beloved. It cannot be otherwise; love cannot be neutral, even though it may be willing to sacrifice itself regardless of the beloved's response.

Around AD 563, the great Irish saint Columba sailed across the Irish Sea to a small, windswept Scottish island called Iona. There he established a monastery that would become the base for evangelical mission, which would light a candle in the midst of Europe's Dark Ages. The flickering flame of that little outpost grew over the next couple of centuries to a blaze that illuminated countries as far away as Germany. The Christian faith, not to mention literacy and scholarship, libraries and hospitals—all of which had been wiped out by the same "barbarian" waves of invasion that had destroyed the Roman Empire—were more than restored.

But first, and long before he had any inkling of what the fantastic import of his move would be, Columba had to let go. He was the shining light of a prominent family that had included at least one High King of Ireland; he had been a leading scholar at a succession of monastic schools, including the famed Clonard Abbey, the Harvard or Oxford of its time; and he had established several important monasteries himself.

Columba had to release much that he loved: people, places, institutions, the prestige of his position, even an evidently vital ministry. In their place, he had twelve monkish companions; a wild, cold, wet chunk of rock set in the midst of an angry sea; and the need to build their own home before winter set in.

It seems that, like many of us, Columba was not at first inclined to let go willingly. Tradition has it that a theological wrangle loosened his grip: he was offered the choice of excommunication or exile. He wasn't a young man, either, by the standards of the time. At fortysomething, he would have been considered elderly—although he was granted a second wind and lasted another thirty-plus years.

Leaving behind almost all he loved had not been his choice; but Columba accepted his losses as God's calling and spoke often to the other monks of embracing that call joyfully. Instead of losing himself in bitterness, he turned the attention of his heart outward, actively loving the recalcitrant Picts of northern Scotland. He established the area's only center for literacy, preached the gospel, founded several churches, became the diplomat local pagan kings turned to for help in resolving disputes, and developed the little monastery on Iona into a school for missionaries who would carry the good news of God's love deeper and deeper into Britain and the Continent.

But first, he had to let go.

We, too, must open our hearts to release the people, places, and things we love. Not to dismiss them, but so our love does not constrict them, and so they do not keep us from loving more freely and more broadly.

When my eldest son, Caleb, was eight or nine years old, a stray

German Shepherd mutt followed him home one day. (So he said; I suspect there may have been some inducements involved.) The dog appeared to have escaped an equipment yard or farm, for she had no tags or markings except a leather collar that appeared to be much older than she was. She was wary of people, unfamiliar with being petted, seemed never to have been inside a house, and had no idea whatsoever what to do with stairs.

We already had a dog, and one was plenty. It was decreed therefore that Rockie, as Caleb called her, could stay for a couple of weeks, no more, while we found her original owner or another home. She lived with us eleven years.

At first she would take off each time an open gate or door gave her a glimpse of freedom. We would chase her and call her and eventually corral her. It was tedious, and the dog remained timid and uncertain toward us.

One day, as our entire family was out in the front yard, Rockie slipped her chain somehow and took off down the street. Caleb and his brother Jesse leapt up and began to run after her, but I called them back.

"Let her go," I said. "Let's just see what happens." I had a hunch.

The kids watched her anxiously as she galloped along the sidewalk away from us. After she had gone thirty or forty yards, she slowed to a trot and cast a doggy glance over her shoulder. She did this a couple of more times, and realizing we weren't following, she slowed further to a walking pace. About sixty yards out, Rockie stopped, turned to face us, and sat down.

The children and the dog contemplated one another for several seconds, then she stood up, and with an embarrassed look and a lolling tongue, she began to trudge back along the sidewalk toward us.

The children remained right where they were and ultimately welcomed the prodigal home with great joy—with belly rubs and ear scratches and much stroking. From that moment to the day of her death, the farthest Rockie ran when she got loose was from the backyard to the front porch.

Two important things happened when Caleb and Jesse, and the two little ones, Rachel and Kelly, let go of the pet they loved: Rockie discovered she loved them, too, and didn't really want to be separated from them. The children discovered their pooch didn't need to be clung to in order to receive their love. They trusted each other for the first time, and trust is a marvelous and necessary fertilizer in the soil of love.

Columba trusted the loving heart of God, embracing a new life far richer than his previous one. God trusts us to love him—not because he thinks we are all trustworthy, for from the beginning humanity has proven it is not, but because he knows we must be free to choose in order to love him, or it is no love at all.

We, too, must learn to release our grip on that which we love, so our love may truly be loving, and so the people we love may be free to truly love in return. We must find courage to let go in the face of our fear of loss; we need help to become so generously open. So we pray:

Lord, open my heart,
that I may release what I have loved,
and so receive your love for me,
love you more deeply,
and truly love others.

Receiving

Lord, open my heart,
that I may release what I have loved,
and so receive your love for me,
love you more deeply,
and truly love others.

All of us are seeking to be loved. So much so that if we are unable to find real love, we will often accept the merest substitutes in its place: money, alcohol, success, busyness, power, notoriety, recreational sex, dysfunctional relationships—anything that obscures the gaping holes in our hearts. Even when we are in secure, healthy, loving relationships, most of us still need regular reassurance that we are loved.

We are seeking to be loved, and yet nowhere does the Bible encourage us to search for love for ourselves. The Mosaic law commands us to love God and our neighbors as ourselves. Jesus' "new commandment" is that we should love one another.

It is difficult—perhaps impossible—for us to love others unless we know we ourselves are loved. And it is difficult—perhaps impossible—for us to love ourselves unless we believe someone else loves us. God, who made us and expresses his longing to be loved by us, knows this.

We are commanded to love rather than to *be* loved for one simple, profound, and—when it truly gets a hold on us—thrilling reason: *we are already supremely loved.*

God's love for the people he has created, and then redeemed, is the greatest theme of the Bible. Everything in the entire biblical story, spread over thousands of years, points to God's love, one way or another.

Jesus' disciple John was a Jew for whom the biblical story was the air he had breathed since he was an infant; he left his fishnets to follow the Son of God, was present at his Master's crucifixion, witnessed the resurrection, cared for Mary as if she were his own mother, and spent his whole long life thinking and teaching about it all.

John's conclusion: God *is* love.[4]

The awareness that God is loving and not only an awesome

power to be feared and obeyed begins to dawn on the far bank of the Red Sea, as the people are led in a song of relief, joy, and thanksgiving by Miriam and Moses. They sing of how God had not forgotten them during their long years of slavery; how he had pried them loose from the most powerful empire on earth; how he had miraculously rescued them when it seemed certain they would be captured again or slaughtered.

Why would an all-powerful God choose to do all this for a powerless, unimportant group of people, chattel of the Egyptians, who as yet had no sense of nationality, nor anywhere they really belonged? The deities of Egypt would never have even noticed their sorrow. It dawns on the singers that there can only be one reason: *Yahweh, the God who is a warrior, majestic in power, loves us!*

Imagine how these words rang out as the Israelites sang them:

> *In your unfailing love you will lead*
> *the people you have redeemed.*
> *In your strength you will guide them*
> *to your holy dwelling.* (Ex. 15:13)

Later, as Yahweh delivered the law to Moses and provided food, drink, and safety for them as they journeyed through the desert, he himself repeatedly explained his motivation for his care and attention: *because of his great love* for this unruly, fickle mob of former slaves.

The character of this great love is emphasized throughout the Hebrew scriptures by the use of the term *hesed*, often translated *steadfast love*. Throughout the Psalms, it is the invariable term used to describe God's commitment to and affection for his people. In Psalm 136, the phrase "his steadfast love[5] endures forever" is a refrain repeated twenty-six times to underscore God's motivation in creation, his every action in defense and support of his people, and the reason his people praise him.

The Hebrew word is difficult to translate concisely, which is why it gets translated differently in various versions and contexts. It's a love that is unwavering, comprehensive, indestructible, undeflectable, infinitely capacious, merciful, and kind. And—here's a sweet thought!—*hesed* indicates not only the immutability of the love being extended but also that the lover receives something in return. God loves us and *gets something himself out of doing so.*

In the prophetic books, God's love is often characterized as that of a parent reaching out to a wayward child, or a husband tenaciously faithful to a distracted or even unfaithful wife. And then, in the story of Jesus, the expression of God's love reached its apogee as John, the apostle of Love, wrote: "This is how God showed his love among us: He sent his one and only Son into the world that we might live through him. This is love: not that we loved God, but that he loved us" (1 John 4:9–10).

The final biblical image, in the last two chapters of the Revelation, is of God in intimate, loving, eternal relationship with the people he has redeemed. We are pictured as both the bride of Christ and as God's eternal home, the city in which he dwells.

And so those of us who are familiar with and give credence to the great story of the Bible, and especially the self-gift of Jesus, may express ourselves with the words of the prophet Jeremiah:

> The LORD appeared to us in the past, saying:
> "I have loved you with an everlasting love;
> I have drawn you with unfailing kindness."
> (Jer. 31:3)

We may say this; we may acknowledge that God has so spoken and acted toward others; but we may still not feel the reality of it for ourselves. And where love is at issue, feeling is usually what is most important to us. Being convinced in our minds of the doctrines of God's love doesn't always convince our hearts. This is an example of how our hearts command us: if our hearts are not receiving the love God extends to us, what we believe with our minds alone becomes either irrelevant or a cold, rigid dogma instead of a life-giving faith.

Since God is not physically present with us, we don't experience his love in the same way that we do with a human being, who can hug or kiss us or tell us in an audible voice, "I love you." Our struggles, failures, and fears may at times make God and his love for us seem very distant or unrealistic, like a fairy tale.

How then can we actually receive his love for us?

Scientists and philosophers refer to "empirical evidence": truths that may be directly observed or proven by experiment. God's existence, let alone his love for us, cannot be proven empirically. Philosophers and theologians describe experiences, being spiritual in nature and impossible to define, as "numinous." It is here, in the realm of the numinous, that the heart may know what the mind alone is unable to grasp.

This is not a knowledge that may be achieved by gathering facts and submitting them to analysis. We pray that God will open our hearts because we cannot do so for ourselves. God's people's long experience of steadfast love sends echoes of longing through our own hearts, even when they are tightly closed. We do not need to be concerned about whether or not we are or will be loved; we need only have our hearts opened, and his love will come seeping or flooding in.

When our hearts are open, we begin to understand that trouble in our lives is not an indication we are unloved or that God has abandoned us. In fact, we may find it is a gift; that by the means of difficulty and even suffering, God is leading us deeper and deeper into his own heart.

"For the Lord disciplines the one he loves," the writer of the letter to the Hebrews said, as a parent disciplines a beloved child (12:6 ESV); Paul told the Romans that "the sufferings of this present time are not worth comparing with the glory that is to be revealed to us" (Rom. 8:18 ESV).

Thomas Merton wrote, "As long as we are on earth, the love that unites us will bring us suffering by our very contact with one another, because this love is the resetting of a Body of broken bones."[6]

He reminded us that love and suffering are intimately acquainted in our lives, and that, in love, God equates that suffering with the passion of his own beloved Son, whose suffering was prompted by his love for us.

Merton intimated, too, the great truth that since God is the source of all love, every love with which we are loved is his love. Those people who love us, whether deeply or in small, shallow ways; whether with the abiding love of a spouse of many years or the simple affection of a little child; whether they themselves trust in God's love or they deny his very existence: they are all narrow conduits for the broad, rushing tide of the one supreme love. Perhaps it is a grace that God irrigates us with many little trickles of his love; it seems unlikely that our small hearts could stand in the great torrent should he love us more directly.

But if we are not yet able to encompass the love of God in its fullness, we may certainly dwell within it. In the Upper Room, before he went out to be taken and crucified, Jesus encouraged his disciples: "As the Father has loved me, so have I loved you. Abide in my love. If you keep my commandments, you will abide in my love, just as I have kept my Father's commandments and abide in his love" (John 15:9–10).

To *abide* is to stay in one place and make it home. The love of God, expressed by Jesus, is the house in which he invites us to live. We enter this house in faith and make a home there by keeping his commandments, the summation of which is *love one another.*

By our senses, we apprehend the empirical: we see what light reveals, hear actual sounds, inhale smells, eat food, and touch real, material objects. Our minds gather and process knowledge. By them, if our senses and minds are opened by God, we come to a deeper experience of him. But the experience of our hearts may not be so defined. Our hearts apprehend mystery.

With open hearts, we may trace the design of love within suffering, recognize the Great Source of Love behind the flickering and inconstant love of the people nearest us, and find a home within love itself. These mysteries are too great for us to encompass, but with open hearts they may fill us. Because we cannot truly open our hearts in our own strength, we pray:

> Lord, open my heart,
> that I may release what I have loved,
> *and so receive your love for me,*
> love you more deeply,
> and truly love others.

Becoming

> Lord, open my heart,
> that I may release what I have loved,
> and so receive your love for me,
> *love you more deeply,*
> and truly love others.

Do a quick online search for quotes about God and love: you'll find thousands about God loving us, and virtually none about us loving God. Which is odd, since "Love the Lord your God" is the first of the commandments and is reiterated in the Bible as God's commandment, invitation, challenge, encouragement, and really, the nut of his expressed desire for relationship with humanity from beginning to end.

Perhaps this is a facet of our increasingly individualized, selfish world. The old contemplative masters spoke and wrote extensively about loving God, and spent little time trying to convince themselves or others that God loved them. That, as far as they were concerned, was established.

Rabbinical teachers understood from earliest times that the whole of the Mosaic law could be summed up thus: "You shall love the LORD your God with all your heart and with all your soul and with all your might."[7] Repeatedly, throughout the Law, the historical books, the poetic and prophetic books, God clearly enunciates his desire to be loved by the people he loves. It is the core of his agenda. He said it explicitly, couched the message in elaborate metaphor, and pulled the strings of history to make his point unmistakably.

God, it seems, is not keen on having an unrequited love affair with us. He wants us to grow up a little and begin to reciprocate.

In fact, it could be convincingly argued that the purpose of the whole of history, from God's point of view, is to find out who among us will choose to love him back. Despite his "command" that we must love him, he will not force us into relationship with him. Even God must let go of the ones he loves; some will return to him, but many will not. From his perspective, it must be awful, costly, and heartbreaking to see some of those he loves so dearly walk away, but there is no other way.

For those of us who do turn and take a few halting steps along the pathway of love toward our Creator, Savior, and Lover, he empowers our feeble response, magnifies it, blows the smoldering ember into life. If he detects a willingness within us to love him, he begins to strip away the things that distract us.

That, unfortunately, is not always a painless process. My own life sometimes feels as though it has been (and remains) one long, continuous process wherein God pries from my grasp my dependencies, certainties, egocentricity, and various "idols." It's not easy. But it's worth it.

He will one day remove every impediment to loving him and receiving his love. Beyond this life—in posthistory—all we will see will be radiant with the colors of love; the sounds we will hear, the air we will breathe, the food we will taste, the materials we will touch, and the thoughts we will think *will all be love*. The very nature of the world we will inhabit will be love, because we will dwell in God. And it all begins now.

"Whoever abides in love abides in God, and God abides in him" (1 John 4:16 ESV).

Loving God now—even in our halfhearted, sporadic way—is how we begin to acclimatize ourselves for the greater reality that is yet to come.

More than any other thing we do, loving defines us as being human. The act of loving deepens and strengthens our humanity; it does so because it deepens and strengthens our likeness to God. The capacity to love is the seed of the Divine within us. That seed is so richly imbued with life that it can even make godly the lives of people who deny God's existence, but who nevertheless choose to love despite all the dictates of rational self-interest. And loving God is the supreme act of faith.

Loving is how we *become*.

But how, exactly, shall we love God? Loving people is easier, because they are right there in front of us, hoping and needing to be loved. How do we love one who is invisible, untouchable, who has no needs or weaknesses?

Perhaps you have encountered an individual now and then who insists on rattling on about his or her deeply intimate relationship with Jesus; perhaps, like I do, you find yourself ungraciously wondering about that person's emotional stability. (Maybe we're just jealous.) The accounts of some of those medieval mystics of their midnight adoration of the Christ are even more unsettling in their lubricity and difficult for us to relate to.

What, then, can ordinary people like you and me do?

First, we can choose. We *must* choose. We may not know how to love God, but we can choose to say to him, "I want to love you. *Open my heart*—show me how."

And we can attend to the words of Jesus: "If you love me, you will keep my commandments" (John 14:15 ESV).

It's worth noting that Jesus did not say, "Keeping my commandments is how you will love me." I think his point was: if we love him, keeping his commandments or keeping his *words* (as he said a little earlier) will be the natural fruit of that love, much the way trimming the hedge is the natural result of my love for my wife. Or perhaps it's a chicken-and-egg sort of thing, and it doesn't really matter where we start: love him, and we'll end up keeping his words; keep his commandments, and we'll end up loving him.

There are a great many sayings of Jesus recorded in the Gospels that we might construe as his commandments. Let's consider just three together: three imperatives that, if we open our hearts to love God, we can expect to find being enacted in our lives.

Repent;

Remember me;

Love one another.

Repent is a word that has acquired strange associations through the years. It conjures up images of a long-bearded character in a dingy robe carrying a placard, announcing the world's imminent destruction, through the downtown core of a large city. Or a newly convicted criminal, still sitting in the dock, who appears overwhelmed by the enormity of his crime—*repentant*—or not so much—*unrepentant.*

The etymology of our English word *repent* leads us to a Latin root, meaning to regret or to feel sorrow.

Though feeling truly sorry for the bad things we've done and being determined to not do them ever again would certainly make the world a better place if it were more commonly experienced, this is not quite what Jesus meant when he traveled about calling people to "repent, for the kingdom of heaven has come near" (Matt. 4:17).

The word that Jesus and the New Testament writers used, rendered to us in ancient Greek, is made up of two words meaning "beyond" or "after," and "perception or understanding or mind." In common usage, it meant to change one's mind, and so to change direction.

It's not too difficult to imagine Jesus observing our lives and calling out: *Stop a minute, will you? You're running all over, keeping up with your commitments and searching in vain for fulfillment. Stop, right where you are, and turn around. "The kingdom of heaven is near"; here I am, close enough to touch! I've been here all along.*

If we open our hearts to love God, we will find that our attention is slowly drawn from the many distractions in our world; the eyes of our hearts will be enlightened, and we will experience the hope to which he has called us.[8] The direction of our hearts will change; they will turn and face Jesus. Other loves that do not find their root and home in God himself will lose their power. This is *beyond understanding*, and it is real repentance.

As Brother Lawrence wrote, "In order to *know* GOD, we must often *think* of Him; and when we come to *love* Him, we shall then also think of Him often, for our heart will be with our treasure."[9]

This, I think, is what Jesus had in mind when he broke bread and, giving it to his disciples in the Upper Room, said, "Do this in remembrance of me" (Luke 22:19 ESV).

He was saying: Each time you share bread and wine together—every day, in that culture and time—use it as a trigger to deliberately recollect who I am and what I have done. All of it: my birth, my life, the teaching, and miracles. The wonder of Deity made human flesh, sharing every human experience. *I, too, have been hungry and lonely and afraid; rejected and betrayed; I have been poor, homeless, oppressed, beaten, and imprisoned.* Even more astonishing: my willing gift of that body and blood in suffering and death, and my defeat of death itself. My appearances to many after rising again, the words of blessing and commission I spoke, my ascension. *Remember me.*

When our hearts are open to love him, things as common as bread and wine will become reminders of his presence, grace, and beauty. "Our heart will be with our treasure," and the cognizance of its infinite value will grow in us day by day, grace upon grace.

Yesterday, Maggie and I took Otis, our dog, for a walk along the beach. The sand was blanketed with snow; wind and water had built cliffs of shining ice along the shore. The sun was setting behind the city skyline to the west, throwing long pink and purple fingers across the pale-blue shadows on the snow and flicking jewels along the crests of the turquoise waves beyond. A sky high and empty, save for the trembling pastels washing around its rim, lapping up against a bank of cotton batten clouds hunkered on the south shore of Lake Ontario, thirty miles away.

It was more than merely beautiful. I had been praying, *Lord, open my heart, that I may love you more deeply.* God answered: I recollected the One who had spoken this magnificent world into being; my heart turned toward him. More than this I am unable to explain, for the language of my heart in that brief moment was the ineffable language of love. Who can translate it?

Because loving God is beyond our understanding, we pray:

> Lord, open my heart,
> that I may release what I have loved,
> and so receive your love for me,
> *love you more deeply,*
> and truly love others.

Doing

> Lord, open my heart,
> that I may release what I have loved,
> and so receive your love for me,
> love you more deeply,
> *and truly love others.*

John, the apostle of love who described himself in his gospel as "the one whom Jesus loved,"[10] probably lived his final years in the city of Ephesus. Despite having spent years being hounded by the authorities, like the other disciples; having endured exile on the island of Patmos; and having survived being plunged into boiling oil (according to church tradition), John is thought to have eventually died of natural causes, a very old man.

One of his students[11] told of how, toward the end of his life, the old apostle was often carried by the young men to the place where the church met. John had had a long time to think and write and speak about Jesus. He had received and recorded the incredible visions of the Revelation; dictated his own account of the story of the life, teachings, death, and resurrection of his Master, distinctly different in content and tone from the earlier Synoptic Gospels (Matthew, Mark, and Luke); and sent out three short letters in which he distilled what he had learned for the benefit of the church.

As the young men carried him through the streets, John condensed the message still further. "Just love one another," he said to them over and over. "Just love one another."

Loving others, Jesus had taught John, would be the defining mark of his disciples—not moral rectitude, or power, or invincible argument. Loving others was his special, "new" commandment, the singular commandment that both summarized and made sense of all the others. It was how his disciples were to live out the gospel, stepping beyond the familiar boundaries of race and religion, choosing the poor and rejected instead of the rich and influential, until it was said that they had "turned the world upside down" (Acts 17:6 ESV).

Loving others is dangerous in the best possible way.

Loving others, especially those who may be considered "unlovable," is the most radical, and the most practical, of all possible actions. Radical, because doing so returns both the lover and the loved to their rootedness in their Creator regardless of every other determinant of identity, and because it is contrary to all the assumptions and goals of worldly power. Practical, because in the end only love—not politics, or law, or economics, or even theology—can effect true healing, justice, forgiveness, and reconciliation. Only love can bring us to salvation.

Love is the only practicable means of attaining unity. If the congregants of any church began to discuss what, exactly, they understand their agreed-upon statement of faith to mean in its particulars, agreement would fail. If the employees and management of any business were interviewed about the true values of the corporation, as many viewpoints as individuals would be revealed. If activists for justice began to debate social priorities and the best means of attaining them, little unity would be found.

Only love allows us to be truly united and still disagree about matters requiring deep conviction. When religious doctrine, political dogma, and social status are subject to the rule of love, when Christians and Muslims and atheists, conservatives and liberals, rich and poor choose to love across their respective divides, then real, functional unity is possible.

Because of this, love is an implicit threat to the normal power structures of our world, which depend on dominance and division for their existence. And it is a challenge to us as individuals, since there is nothing that makes us more vulnerable than loving someone else. Love challenges everything within us, from ownership to self-image and self-sovereignty; it requires us to face the truth. At times, we may even protect ourselves against being loved by other people, since being loved requires a response.

But such vulnerability is itself a high and Christlike goal, and seeking to become open to it is the true path of faith.

We must remember that the kind of loving to which Jesus calls us is not about having a warm, fuzzy feeling toward others. Nor is it a matter of really liking them a lot. Many of the people in my community struggle with addictions or mental illness or both; there are times when it is difficult to like some of them—and, of course, there are times when they don't like me much either. There are a few individuals I just don't like very much at any time. It's no different for people who work in corporate offices, teach students, or provide services to the public.

But we are not called to like people. We are called to love them.

You have probably heard of the Greek word for this Christlike love, *agape*. We could wax poetic about what it means, but essentially it's about seeking another's good, even when there is cost to your own person. It's actually simpler to love in this way than it is to like everyone or agree with them completely. We can enact this Jesus love even when we dislike and disagree with the person, or when we have no feelings about or for the person at all. It's not easy to love like this, of course—and it's certainly easier if we *do* have some affection for the person and share at least some perspective— but it *is* simple: seek his or her good.

I am an introvert whose daily life is full of people. If, like me, you find the mere thought of actively loving more people than you already do exhausting, don't panic. We are asking God to open our hearts, to shift the direction of our hearts toward him and toward others. God will do this work, not us; his love is inexhaustible. When his love is at work within us, it pours more into us than can be drained out.

Toward whom can we expect that he will direct us?

"Love the sojourner, therefore, for you were sojourners in the land of Egypt," says the Law (Deut. 10:19 ESV). Seek the good of the one who doesn't belong, who is oppressed, excluded, hungry, homeless. In doing so, we recognize the reflection of our own faces in those of the sojourner and are reminded that our love for others is possible because of God's love for us. Jesus added, as we have already seen from Matthew 25, that when we do so, we are also loving him.

"You shall love your neighbor as your self" (Matt. 22:39 ESV; Mark 12:31 ESV). This is how Jesus summarized all the commandments following the first and greatest, "Love the Lord your God with all your heart and with all your soul and with all your mind" (Matt. 22:37). With his story of the good Samaritan, he pointed out that a neighbor is not necessarily someone who lives next door or a person of the same cultural community. Anyone in need is my neighbor.

John, who repeatedly enjoined us to "love one another," in one phrase interprets the words of Jesus in a way that both broadens the scope of loving still further, rendering its imperative in more intimate terms: "This commandment we have from him: whoever loves God must also love his brother" (1 John 4:21 ESV).

Our instinct is to love the ones closest to us—our families and intimate friends—and build a wall around them. John smashed down the wall, calling the stranger, neighbor, and even enemy his brother, just as Jesus did. Loving God reveals that all humanity is beloved of God, that all men, women, and children are kin. And we cannot love God without loving our kin.[12] We keep our eyes open, gazing around us for the ones who seem the most extravagantly other, and recognize in them our sister, our brother.

Our own personal needs are enormous. The needs of a love-starved world around us are overwhelming. God's love, within which we are making a home, and which is making its home within us, is spacious and expansive. Resolving these conundrums is beyond us; and *doing* more, making more space in lives already jammed with people and activities, seems impossible.

We need to rest. Rest. Rest in the arms of the One who is love, trusting that his plans for us are love. Trusting that loving people equals loving God equals loving people. Our little hearts long to swim in a love this deep and wide, and so we invite him:

Lord, open my heart,
that I may release what I have loved,
and so receive your love for me,
love you more deeply,
and truly love others.

Remember . . .

- *The heart has ways of knowing that the mind cannot compute.*

- *A love that opens its arms, including instead of excluding, will find its resource deepens and expands; it will become both stronger and more tender.*

- *We are commanded to love rather than to be loved for one simple, profound, and thrilling reason: we are already supremely loved.*

- *When our hearts are open to love God, things as common as bread and wine will become reminders of his presence, grace, and beauty.*

- *Loving others is the defining mark of Jesus' disciples.*

For Examen (reflection or discussion)

- *Is there something, or someone, you love that you sense you must release? Does the thought of doing so frighten you?*

- *Within your own life experience, or within the experiences of the last day or two, can you "trace the design of God's love" for you?*

- *What presents the greatest challenge for you in loving God? Has your heart turned toward him in some way today?*

- *Is there "another" whom you sense God is calling you to love?*

9

Onward

We have come to the end of our description of what we might encounter along this contemplative path; but we have not, of course, come to an end of the path itself. As we desire to continue to become more and more open to God, ourselves, and others over the entire course, so we hope that our simple prayer will weave itself into the fabric of our lives.

Although I have described the path to openness in a linear fashion—moving through the five senses, mind, and heart sequentially, and in each through the cycle of *releasing, receiving, becoming,* and *doing*—the further along the path we get, the more we will find that it is not linear or sequential at all.

We will find that inhaling a particular fragrance, and receiving it as a gift of God's Spirit, will cause us to see or hear something differently; we may realize that we need to let go of a certain way of thinking, and thus find our hearts drawn to loving someone previously unnoticed. Our senses, minds, and hearts are, after all, beautifully integrated within our unique selves.

Still, it may be a helpful discipline to patiently pray our way along each portion of this path in the order given, or at least to commit ourselves to praying for openness in a specific way (one of the senses, our minds, or hearts) for a period of time. A more random approach may become difficult to sustain.

Isn't it interesting that we always say "open up" and never "open down"? Two people sit on a bench, one staring at the ground between her feet and the other with his head thrown back, face turned to the sky. Which posture seems to indicate an open spirit? I wonder if, instinctively, we sense that openness is a gift from above.

It's important to simply receive this gift without complicating it too much—an inevitable tendency of human beings. Beyond asking God to open us up, and later asking ourselves how he has done so, we don't need to try to make anything happen. We will almost certainly find God leading us in new directions as a result.

Our desire to become so simply open is a matter of our spirits answering the Spirit: we sense that God himself is open. And because he is, we can be confident he will answer our prayer—even if, as I found on the path to Quarr, we must walk a few miles before we realize that he is answering.

Later, as I reflected on my time on the Isle of Wight and remembered ruefully how long it took me to see something so obvious and near at hand, the simple word *open* seemed to grow in importance. A true openness would have helped me more easily see and receive what was being offered.

And the more I thought about it, the more it seemed to me that *seeing* was mostly about becoming *open*, rather than the reverse.

I thought about the many ways I had simply enjoyed being there—listening to the singing of the monks, the cries of the birds, the lapping of the ocean against the shore; the taste of good British ale and the buttered scone I ordered each day at the tea shop; the smell of blossoms and kelp drying on the rocks; the feel of the pews in the old Norman church, polished by the hands and bodies of generations of parishioners; and the gentle rain on my face in early morning.

> Look, I tell you, lift up your eyes, and see
> that the fields are white for harvest.
> He who has ears to hear, let him hear.
> For we are the aroma of Christ to God.
> Oh, taste and see that the LORD is good!
> Touch me, and see. For a spirit does not have
> flesh and bones as you see that I have.[1]

No matter where we are, no matter what we're doing, no matter how busy we get, our senses are engaged—even when we are largely unconscious of them. Scripture makes it abundantly clear, as does personal experience at some level for almost everyone, that our five senses, along with our minds and hearts, provide a path deeper into the great mystery of God.[2] The world around us—even our cities, which are largely constructed and constrained by human effort—is redolent with that mystery.

God the Unknowable desires to be known. It is this confidence that gives our prayer for openness substance. Everywhere and always, he is proclaiming himself, but the mysteries of God are a limitless landscape: mountains and plains, desert and jungle, city and deep forest. We never reach the horizon.

The deeper we trek into these mysteries, the less we are bound by the mundaneness of our proximate reality; the truer and bigger and more limitless—if it's possible for something to be *more* limitless—the mystery is revealed to be. This mystery is not mysterious because it is hidden, or because it desires to remain a secret open only to the few, but because its hugeness cannot be encompassed. The small, discernable pieces of it may be separated by such wide distances within the mystery that we are unable to make the innumerable incremental connections between them; but we must be content, for now, with paradox.

We cannot contain; we can only be open.

Our knowing of God and his mysteries cannot be restricted only to rational process—although rational processes can't be dismissed either. A great many of the mysteries being revealed to us are as material and measurable as light or sound or the force of gravity. But many other mysteries are knowable only experientially, and we investigate them by means of our five senses, our minds, and our hearts.

How do I know that the breeze playing over my face is the very breath of God? This is not rational, although neither is it irrational. It is, perhaps, extra-rational. At any rate, I know the feel of the breath of God by a thousand indefinable means; it is this very indefinability, this mystery, that confirms my knowing.

The sheer scale of the landscape of mysteries is daunting. We could lose ourselves in it. We would often rather call a puddle *God*—we would rather encompass God than have him encompass us. This impulse is the source of restrictive dogmas and theological systems; it's also, I think, the reason some are unable or unwilling to believe there is a God at all.

Never mind the puddle. Come—let's lose ourselves in the wide-open world of his grace.

Acknowledgments

This book would be only a set of half-formed ideas rattling around in my mind without the support and input of a great many people.

Miller and Terri Alloway have been generous patrons for years, providing time, space, and financial support that has afforded me the luxury of focusing on writing free from distraction. Tim Huff, my writing buddy, has walked the path with me while working on his own excellent books.

Greg Daniel helped shape the concept of the book and found a home for it. The editing team at Thomas Nelson—Jocelyn Bailey, Janene MacIvor, and especially Joel Miller—challenged, trimmed, and even added, until *Simply Open* was as good as it was ever going to get. Brian Hampton was willing to gamble on me again, and I'm grateful for his confidence.

As always, the Sanctuary community is the main source (after God) of what is offered in these pages. The board grants me the mandate and time to write; the staff keeps me connected with the rest of the community and exemplifies what Christian life ought to look like; my street-involved brothers and sisters are the greatest spiritual teachers I have ever had. Dan, Les, and Doug have been band mates and fellow travelers for almost thirty years.

Having quoted contemplative writers will serve as my

acknowledgment of the great debt I, and many others, owe to them. Likewise, the friends and influencers I have mentioned in the book, as well as too many to list whom I have not.

My four children—Caleb, Jesse, Rachel, and Kelly—have been unconsciously involved in shaping my spiritual character and perspective for more than thirty years. By their love, and now their adult friendship, they continue that work. These last few years, my wife's children—Cam, Reid, and Gilly—have begun to do the same.

And finally, there's Maggie. Closest friend, most intimate companion, exemplar of openness, agent of God's healing in my soul, sweetest love. The Great Openness beckons. Take my hand . . .

Notes

Chapter 1: The Path to Openness

1. More accurately, the Low Income Cut-Off: the point at which sociologists and economists have agreed a family can actually feed, clothe, and house themselves in a relatively stable fashion. "Poverty by Postal Code," a 2004 report prepared jointly by United Way of Greater Toronto and the Canadian Council on Social Development; Executive Summary, 16.

2. For more on St. Simeon Stylites, see "St Simeon Stylites, the Elder," *Orthodox Church in America*, http://oca.org/saints /lives/2014/09/01/102448-st-simeon-stylites-the-elder.

3. The Sanctuary community in Toronto, my home, is both strangely holy and extraordinarily profane. For more on Sanctuary Ministries, see http://www.sanctuarytoronto.ca or Greg Paul, *The Twenty-Piece Shuffle: Why the Poor and Rich Need Each Other* (Colorado Springs: David C. Cook, 2006).

4. Arthur Paul Boers and Eugene H. Peterson, *The Way Is Made by Walking: A Pilgrimage Along the Camino de Santiago* (Downers Grove, IL: IVP Books, 2007).

5. Arthur Boers, *Living into Focus: Choosing What Matters in an Age of Distraction* (Grand Rapids, MI: Brazos Press, 2012).

6. This is a rather simplistic description of Examen. If you're interested, you could pick up a copy of *The Spiritual Exercises of St. Ignatius of Loyola*, trans. Anthony Mottola (New York: Doubleday, 1989).

7. Some scholars say that this is what Chinese sage Lao-tzu was getting at with his saying that is more popularly rendered, "The longest journey begins with a single step."

Chapter 2: Open My Eyes

1. Robert H. Spector, *Clinical Methods: The History, Physical, and Laboratory Examinations*, 3rd edition (1990). Also, http://www.ncbi.nlm.nih.gov/books/NBK220/.
2. Boonsri Dickinson, "Eyes May Really Be the Window to the Soul," *Discover*, May 17, 2007, http://discovermagazine.com/2007/may/eyes-may-really-be-the-window-to-the-soul.
3. Richard Rohr, *Everything Belongs: The Gift of Contemplative Prayer* (New York: Crossroad Publishing, 1999), 67.
4. Isaiah 52:14–53:3, paraphrased.
5. Specifically, Paul is referring to the Law of Moses. He is saying that the paradigm created by Mosaic law and the centuries of rabbinical comment attached to it have created a barrier to seeing God clearly—a problem Moses himself did not have.
6. Consider the Song of Solomon, a passionate and frankly erotic poem that commentators, both Jewish and Christian, from every era have understood as an expression of the love relationship between God and his people; or the various descriptions in Revelation of the relationship between Christ and the church as that of a groom and bride.
7. Not all biblical commentators believe that the four accounts (Matt. 26:6–13; Mark 14:3–9; Luke 7:36–50; John 12:1–8) are all about the same actual event, although it's certainly possible. At any rate, the essential story is the same in all four accounts.

Chapter 3: Open My Ears

1. "Sensitivity of Human Ear," *HyperPhysics*, Georgia State University, http://hyperphysics.phy-astr.gsu.edu/hbase/sound/earsens.html.
2. Thomas Merton, "Rain and the Rhinoceros," *Raids on the Unspeakable* (New York: New Directions, 1966), 10.
3. Isaiah 40:21 (ESV).
4. Jeremiah 17:23 (ESV), and a great many other places.
5. Kenneth E. Bailey, *Jesus Through Middle Eastern Eyes: Cultural Studies in the Gospels* (Downers Grove, IL: InterVarsity Press, 2008), 93.
6. John Donne and Henry Alford, *Works of John Donne, D.D., Dean of Saint Paul's, 1621–1631, With a Memoir of His Life* (London: John W. Parker, 1839), 3:477.

7. Thomas à Kempis, *Of the Imitation of Christ: Four Books* (Oxford: James Parker and Co., 1869), 12.
8. Thomas Merton, *New Seeds of Contemplation* (New York: New Directions, 1961), 2.
9. Ibid., xvi.
10. Ezekiel 3:3; Jeremiah 15:16.
11. Greg Paul, *Close Enough to Hear God Breathe: The Great Story of Divine Intimacy* (Nashville: Thomas Nelson, 2011). This book shows how, through the entire sweep of the biblical story, God speaks a consistent message to us: we are his children, he loves us, and he's pleased with us.
12. Henri J. M. Nouwen, *The Inner Voice of Love* (New York: Doubleday, 1996), 6.
13. Henri J. M. Nouwen, *The Wounded Healer: Ministry in Contemporary Society* (New York: Doubleday, 1972).
14. Merton, *New Seeds of Contemplation*, 37.
15. Mark 7:32–35.
16. Job 42:3.
17. John 1:1–5.
18. Hebrews 1:3.
19. Deuteronomy 15:9; 24:14–15; James 5:1–4.
20. http://www.personal-coaching-information.com/levels-of-listening.html.

Chapter 4: Open My Nostrils

1. For the sake of simplicity on our contemplative path, I have somewhat arbitrarily considered breathing only as a function of our nostrils and not of our mouths.
2. The Hebrew word *ru'ach* literally means wind, and by extension, breath and spirit. The Greek *pneuma* also means breath, a blast of air (think pneumatic drill or wrench), and spirit.
3. Meghan Holohan, "Smells Like Nostalgia: Why Do Scents Bring Back Memories?" *NBCNews.com*, July 19, 2012, http://www.nbcnews.com/health/body-odd/smells-nostalgia-why-do-scents-bring-back-memories-f895521.
4. St. Teresa of Ávila, *Interior Castle*, ed. and trans. E. Allison Peers (Mineola, NY: Dover, 2007), 93.

Chapter 5: Open My Mouth

1. "The Multiple Dimensions of Food Security," *Food and Agriculture Organization of the United Nations*, 2014, http://www.fao.org /publications/sofi/en/.
2. W. F. Boron and E. L. Boulpaep, *Medical Physiology*, 1st ed. (Elsevier Science USA, 2003).
3. Harvard Sitkoff, *King: Pilgrimage to the Mountaintop* (New York: Hill and Wang, 2008), 207.
4. Alaina McConnell, "Ranked: The Most Popular Fast Food Restaurants in America," *BusinessInsider.com*, July 12, 2013, http://www.businessinsider.com/the-most-popular-fast-food -restaurants-in-america-2012-7?op=1.
5. Thomas à Kempis, *Of the Imitation of Christ: Four Books* (Oxford: James Parker and Co., 1869), 82.
6. Song of Solomon 4:16–5:1 (ESV); 7:8–10 (NIV).
7. Thomas Merton, *New Seeds of Contemplation* (New York: New Directions, 1961), 65–66.
8. Ibid., 143–44.

Chapter 6: Open My Hands

1. Midrash Ecclesiastes Rabbah 5:21. Rabbi Meir was a sage of the Mishnah—the earliest major written redaction of Hebrew oral traditions and the first major work of Rabbinic literature. Circa AD 200.
2. Any number of websites describe versions of this trap, as used by park rangers in Africa and monkey hunters in India, for example. While it's hard to authenticate the monkey trap definitively, this YouTube video shows an African bushman catching a monkey for the purposes of finding a water source: https://www.youtube .com/watch?v=NxkvY2FZRQg.
3. Although we believe that Jesus was and is God, and so would never fail the test, there can be little doubt that the trials and temptations he suffered were real, immediate, and as difficult as they are for us. If this were not so, the words of Hebrews 2:10–18 and 5:7–8 are meaningless, and the Gospel accounts of his temptation in the wilderness seem almost pointless.
4. Philippians 2:6 (ESV).

5. The only other place in the New Testament this term is used is in Romans 1:20, whence also the phrase "his eternal power and divine nature." There, the NIV translates it to "what has been made."

6. Henri J. M. Nouwen, *The Return of the Prodigal Son* (New York: Doubleday, 1992).

7. 2 Timothy 4:5.

Chapter 7: Open My Mind

1. Nicholas Rescher, *G. W. Leibniz's Monadology* (New York: Routledge, 1991), 83.

2. *We Believe in One God*, ed. Gerald L. Bray (Downers Grove, IL: InterVarsity Press, 2009), 50.

3. Michael Ruse, *Science and Spirituality: Making Room for Faith in the Age of Science* (New York: Cambridge UP, 2010), 3.

4. *Einstein for the 21st Century: His Legacy in Science, Art, and Modern Culture*, eds. Peter L. Galison, Gerald Holton, and Silvan S. Schweber (Princeton: Princeton UP, 2008), 37.

5. Max Jammer, *Einstein and Religion: Physics and Theology* (Princeton: Princeton UP, 1999), 157.

6. Sir Isaac Newton, *Newton's Principia: The Mathematical Principles of Natural Philosophy*, trans. Andrew Motte (New York: Daniel Adee, 1848), 35, 506.

7. *Einstein for the 21st Century*, 222.

8. J. A. Leo Lemay, *The Life of Benjamin Franklin, Volume 2: Printer and Publisher, 1730–1747* (Philadelphia: University of Pennsylvania Press, 2006), 205.

9. C. S. Lewis, *Letters to Malcolm: Chiefly on Prayer* (New York: Harcourt Brace & World, 1964), 34.

10. Thomas à Kempis, *Of the Imitation of Christ: Four Books* (Oxford: James Parker and Co., 1869), 2–3.

11. Søren Kierkegaard, *Søren Kierkegaard's Journals and Papers*, trans. Howard V. Hong and Edna H. Hong (Bloomington: Indiana University Press, 1967), 5:59.

12. C. G. Jung, "America: The Pueblo Indians," *Memories, Dreams, Reflections*, ed. Aniela Jaffé, trans. Richard and Clara Winston (New York: Vintage Books, 1989), IX.ii.

Chapter 8: Open My Heart

1. Luke 24:13–35.
2. 1 Corinthians 13.
3. 1 John 4:20.
4. 1 John 4:8–16.
5. ESV, *steadfast love*; KJV, *mercy*; NASB, *lovingkindness*.
6. Thomas Merton, *New Seeds of Contemplation* (New York: New Directions, 1961), 72.
7. Deuteronomy 6:5 and several other places, including Matthew 22:37, where Jesus himself made exactly this point.
8. Ephesians 1:18.
9. Brother Lawrence, *The Practice of the Presence of God* (Radford, VA: Wilder, 2008), 48.
10. John 20:2; also 13:23; 21:7; and 21:20.
11. Irenaeus, a bishop of Lugdunum (now Lyons, France) and second-century apologist who wrote a number of books, recorded this story as told to him by Polycarp, a disciple of John's during the last twenty years of his life. Polycarp became bishop of Smyrna and was eventually martyred.
12. 1 John 4:20.

Chapter 9: Onward

1. John 4:35; Matthew 11:15; 2 Corinthians 2:15; Psalm 34:8; Luke 24:39 (all ESV).
2. Try doing a biblical word search with terms like *eyes, see, ear, hear, mouth, lips, taste, nostrils, breathe, hand,* or *touch.* You'll find thousands of references.

About the Author

G reg Paul is a pastor and member of the Sanctuary community in Toronto. Sanctuary, a community in which people who are wealthy and people who are poor live, work, and share their experiences and resources on a daily basis, makes a priority of welcoming and caring for some of the most hurting and excluded people in the city, including addicts; prostitutes; homeless men, women, and youth; and gay, lesbian, and transgendered people.

(www.sanctuarytoronto.ca)

A former carpenter, Greg has been involved in inner-city ministry since his teen years. He is the father of four children and husband to Maggie, who has three children of her own. He is the author of three other books: *Close Enough to Hear God Breathe, The Twenty-Piece Shuffle,* and *God in the Alley.*

Follow Greg on Twitter @GregPaul58